POPULAR
MUSIC

The Popular Music Series

Popular Music, 1980–1989 is a revised cumulation of and supersedes Volumes 9 through 14 of the *Popular Music* series, all of which are still available:

Volume 9, 1980–84
Volume 10, 1985
Volume 11, 1986

Volume 12, 1987
Volume 13, 1988
Volume 14, 1989

Popular Music, 1920–1979 is also a revised cumulation of and supersedes Volumes 1 through 8 of the *Popular Music* series, of which Volumes 6 through 8 are still available:

Volume 1, 2nd ed., 1950–59
Volume 2, 1940–49
Volume 3, 1960–64
Volume 4, 1930–39

Volume 5, 1920–29
Volume 6, 1965–69
Volume 7, 1970–74
Volume 8, 1975–79

Popular Music, 1900–1919 is a companion volume to the revised cumulation.

This series continues with:

Volume 15, 1990
Volume 16, 1991
Volume 17, 1992

Volume 18, 1993
Volume 19, 1994

Other Books by Bruce Pollock

The Face of Rock and Roll: Images of a Generation

Hipper Than Our Kids?: A Rock and Roll Journal of the Baby Boom Generation

In Their Own Words: Popular Songwriting, 1955–1974

When Rock Was Young: The Heyday of Top 40

When the Music Mattered: Rock in the 1960s

ISSN 0886-442X

VOLUME 19

1994

POPULAR MUSIC

An Annotated Guide to American Popular Songs,
cluding Introductory Essays, Lyricists and Composers Index,
Important Performances Index, Chronological Index,
Awards Index, and List of Publishers

BRUCE POLLOCK
Editor

 *Gale Research Inc.*

An International Thomson Publishing Company

I(T)P

NEW YORK • LONDON • BONN • BOSTON • DETROIT • MADRID
MELBOURNE • MEXICO CITY • PARIS • SINGAPORE • TOKYO
TORONTO • WASHINGTON • ALBANY NY • BELMONT CA • CINCINNATI OH

Bruce Pollock, *Editor*

Gale Research Inc. Staff

Jolen Marya Gedridge, *Associate Editor*
Lawrence W. Baker, *Managing Editor*

Mary Beth Trimper, *Production Director*
Deborah L. Milliken, *Production Assistant*

Cynthia Baldwin, *Production Design Manager*
Barbara J. Yarrow, *Graphic Services Supervisor*

Theresa Rocklin, *Manager, Technical Support Services*
Charles Beaumont, Sheila Printup, and Neil Yee, *Programmers/Analysts*
Benita L. Spight, Manager, *Data Entry Services*
Rhonda A. Willis, *Data Entry Supervisor*
Gwendolyn S. Tucker, *Data Entry Coordinator*
Lysandra C. Davis, Kweli K. Jomo, and Arlene Ann Kevonian, *Data Entry Associates*

∞™ This book is printed on acid-free paper that meets the minimum requirements of American National Standard for Information Sciences—Permanence Paper for Printed Library Materials, ANSI Z39.48-1984.

Library of Congress Catalog Card Number 85-653754
ISBN 0-8103-9057-4
ISSN 0886-442X

I(T)P™
The trademark ITP is used under license.
10 9 8 7 6 5 4 3 2 1

Contents

About the Book and How to Use It

This volume is the nineteenth of a series whose aim is to set down in permanent and practical form a selective, annotated list of the significant popular songs of our times. Other indexes of popular music have either dealt with special areas, such as jazz or theater and film music, or been concerned chiefly with songs that achieved a degree of popularity as measured by the music-business trade indicators, which vary widely in reliability.

Annual Publication Schedule

The first nine volumes in the *Popular Music* series covered sixty-five years of song history in increments of five or ten years. Volume 10 initiated a new annual publication schedule, making background information available as soon as possible after a song achieves prominence. Yearly publication also allows deeper coverage—approximately five hundred songs—with additional details about writers' inspiration, uses of songs, album appearances, and more.

Indexes Provide Additional Access

Three indexes make the valuable information in the song listings even more accessible to users. The Lyricists & Composers Index shows all the songs represented in *Popular Music, 1994,* that are credited to a given individual. The Important Performances Index tells at a glance which albums, musicals, films, television shows, or other media-featured songs are represented in the volume. The "Performer" category—first added to the index as "Vocalist" in the 1986 volume—allows the user to see with which songs an artist has been associated this year. The index is arranged by broad media category, then alphabetically by the show or album title, with the songs listed under each title. Finally, the Awards Index provides a list of the songs nominated for awards by the American Academy of Motion Picture Arts and Sciences (Academy Award) and the American Academy of Recording Arts and Sciences (Grammy Award). Winning songs are indicated by asterisks.

About the Book and How to Use It

List of Publishers

The List of Publishers is an alphabetically arranged directory providing addresses—when available—for the publishers of the songs represented in *Popular Music, 1994*. Also noted is the organization handling performance rights for the publisher—in the United States, the American Society of Composers, Authors, and Publishers (ASCAP) or Broadcast Music, Inc. (BMI); in Canada, the Society of Composers, Authors, and Music Publishers of Canada (SOCAN); and in Europe, the Society of European Songwriters and Composers (SESAC).

Tracking Down Information on Songs

Unfortunately, the basic records kept by the active participants in the music business are often casual, inaccurate, and transitory. There is no single source of comprehensive information about popular songs, and those sources that do exist do not publish complete material about even the musical works with which they are directly concerned. Four of the primary proprietors of basic information about our popular music are the major performing rights societies—ASCAP, BMI, SOCAN, and SESAC. Although each of these organizations has considerable information about the songs of its own writer and publisher members and has also issued indexes of its own songs, their files and published indexes are designed primarily for clearance identification by the commercial users of music. Their publications of annual or periodic lists of their "hits" necessarily include only a small fraction of their songs, and the facts given about these are also limited. ASCAP, BMI, SOCAN, and SESAC are, however, invaluable and indispensable sources of data about popular music. It is just that their data and special knowledge are not readily accessible to the researcher.

Another basic source of information about musical compositions and their creators and publishers is the Copyright Office of the Library of Congress. A computerized file lists each published, unpublished, republished, and renewed copyright of songs registered with the Office. It takes between six months and a year from the time of application before songs are officially registered (in some cases, songs have already been released before copyright registration begins). This file is helpful in determining the precise date of the declaration of the original ownership of musical works, but since some authors, composers, and publishers have been known to employ rather makeshift methods of protecting their works legally, there are songs listed in *Popular Music* that may not be found in the Library of Congress files.

About the Book and How to Use It

Selection Criteria

In preparing the original volumes for this time period, the editor was faced with a number of separate problems. The first and most important of these was that of selection. The stated aim of the project—to offer the user as comprehensive and accurate a listing of significant popular songs as possible—has been the guiding criterion. The purpose has never been to offer a judgment on the quality of any songs or to indulge a prejudice for or against any type of popular music. Rather, it is the purpose of *Popular Music* to document those musical works that (1) achieved a substantial degree of popular acceptance, (2) were exposed to the public in especially notable circumstances, or (3) were accepted and given important performances by influential musical and dramatic artists.

Another problem was whether or not to classify the songs as to type. Most works of music are subject to any number of interpretations and, although it is possible to describe a particular performance, it is more difficult to give a musical composition a label applicable not only to its origin but to its subsequent musical history. In fact, the most significant versions of some songs are often quite at variance with their origins. Citations for such songs in *Popular Music* indicate the important facts about not only their origins but also their subsequent lives, rather than assigning an arbitrary and possibly misleading label.

Research Sources

The principal sources of information for the titles, authors, composers, publishers, and dates of copyright of the songs in this volume were the Copyright Office of the Library of Congress, ASCAP, BMI, SOCAN, SESAC, and individual writers and publishers. Data about best-selling recordings were obtained principally from three of the leading music business trade journals—*Billboard, Radio & Records,* and *Cash Box.* For the historical notes; information about foreign, folk, public domain, and classical origins; and identification of theatrical, film, and television introducers of songs, the editor relied upon collections of album notes, theater programs, sheet music, newspaper and magazine articles, and other material, both his own and that in the Lincoln Center Library for the Performing Arts in New York City.

Contents of a Typical Entry

The primary listing for a song includes

- Title and alternate title(s)
- Country of origin (for non-U.S. songs)

- Author(s) and composer(s)
- Current publisher, copyright date
- Annotation on the song's origins or performance history

Title: The full title and alternate title or titles are given exactly as they appear on the Library of Congress copyright record or, in some cases, the sheet music. Since even a casual perusal of the book reveals considerable variation in spelling and punctuation, it should be noted that these are the colloquialisms of the music trade. The title of a given song as it appears in this series is, in almost all instances, the one under which it is legally registered.

Foreign Origin: If a song is of foreign origin, the primary listing indicates the country of origin after the title. Additional information may be noted, such as the original title, copyright date, writer, publisher in country of origin, or other facts about the adaptation.

Authorship: In all cases, the primary listing reports the author or authors and the composer or composers. The reader may find variations in the spelling of a songwriter's name. This results from the fact that some writers used different forms of their names at different times or in connection with different songs. In addition to this kind of variation in the spelling of writers' names, the reader will also notice that in some cases, where the writer is also the performer, the name as a writer may differ from the form of the name used as a performer.

Publisher: The current publisher is listed. Since *Popular Music* is designed as a practical reference work rather than an academic study, and since copyrights more than occasionally change hands, the current publisher is given instead of the original holder of the copyright. If a publisher has, for some reason, copyrighted a song more than once, the years of the significant copyright subsequent to the year of the original copyright are also listed after the publisher's name.

Annotation: The primary listing mentions significant details about the song's history—the musical, film, or other production in which the song was introduced or featured and, where important, by whom it was introduced, in the case of theater and film songs; any other performers identified with the song; first or best-selling recordings and album inclusions, indicating the performer and the record company; awards; and other relevant data. The name of a performer may be listed differently in connection with different songs, especially over a period of years. The name listed is the form of the name given in connection with a particular performance or record. Dates are provided for important recordings and performances.

Popular Music in 1994

Historically, rock eras announce themselves around mid-decade. Starting in 1955, forty years of pop music began to be systematically erased by the appearance of the rockabilly and rhythm and blues hordes led by Elvis Presley, who created rock and roll. In the mid-'60s, with rock and roll firmly co-opted and corporatized into near-oblivion, the protest movement of folk joined hands with the revivified rockabilly and reinvented rhythm and blues of the English invasion to give birth to an underground so vast and hungry that FM radio had to be discovered to service the new genre: rock music.

Around 1975 or so, with the album-buying rock market inspired by FM radio having grown as fat and irrelevant as the Bandstand graduates who preceded them, punk rock exploded onto the scene, in tandem with its slightly more educated cousin, New Wave. But while individual groups achieved outsized success, the New Wave and Punk scenes of the '70s, representing a younger, relatively miniscule demographic, never crashed through radio's then-lock on the populace: classic corporate rock guitar, the mellow singer/songwriter, and the dreaded scourge of disco.

Fast forward another decade, not many years past the arrival of television as the main purveyor of rock's newest stylistic wrinkles. With recycled Led Zeppelin riffs moving into their second decade of squelching the brainpods of another generation on FM radio, MTV's role by the mid-'80s was to reveal and present the alternative. However, with burgeoning video and audio technology skipping hand in hand with the fashion mavens and image consultants of corporate rock's biggest budgets, the post-modern sounds of the Replacements, Soul Asylum, Hüsker Dü, the Dead Kennedys, the Minutemen, and Black Flag, were deemed too unphotogenic and too undercapitalized to represent the underground. We settled for Madonna, Boy George, and Duran Duran—a dressed-up, synthesizer-based Disco Age.

Alternative Meets Mainstream

Thus, after nearly 20 years of a mainstream dominated by corporate rock on the one side (Zeppelin clones) and corporate dance on the other (Madonna wannabees), the mid-'90s have finally seen an underground movement of merit and demographic clout take hold. When the main-

Popular Music in 1994

stream briefly embraced the sounds of alternative rock on the top forty, late in 1993, it represented more than a mere passing of the guard. Just as underground Bob Dylan met the overground Beatles to emerge more like a Rolling Stone in the mid-'60s, the jangly anguished sound of modern rock achieved its mid-'90s breakthrough by accomplishing a long awaited alliance with its more metal-edged musical brethren in the camps of hard rock. Year-end charts reveal an unprecedented merger of bands and songs represented on both.

Throughout 1994, an entire underground was revealed to be sitting there, sweltering, festering, gathering steam—hordes of stripped down psychedelic new wave punk rockers, with exciting, even hummable, guitar driven songs. On the radio, album rock stations and modern rock stations began to get confused, lose their separate identities, play Depeche Mode between Rush and Van Halen, play Green Day, Cracker, and Counting Crows alongside the reunited Plant and Page. Alternative, once the bastion and the ghetto of English and pseudo-English pouting pretty boys, now expanded to include alternative metal, pop, punk, new blues, and anti-folk rap grunge. Most of these records came, as once did the best rock and roll, from feisty and underfinanced independent labels, the old outsider nuzzling up against and spitting on the windowpanes of power that spawned early R&B and rockabilly.

For a generation brought up to treasure irony, the death early in 1994 of Kurt Cobain, lead singer of Nirvana, was a moment where tragedy and symbolism combined to produce a defining epiphany. While a reaction to the cheap kind of overground fame Nirvana was in the process of achieving, Cobain's suicide also wound up not only assuring Nirvana of an endless Doors-like legacy, but it even more quickly advanced the entire alternative movement into the national mainstream spotlight. Of course, the circumstances of his death, coming at his own hand, inevitably evoked the many underground heroes of the '60s who succumbed to drugs, success, and rock and roll.

In 1994, Nirvana's moody laments ("All Apologies," "About a Girl"), were not as accepted on the Top 40 as the janglier alternative of the Gin Blossoms ("Until I Fall Away"), whose 1992 album simply refused to die, even if their original guitarist and songwriter, Doug Hopkins, committed suicide in 1993. Late 1993 entries like "Loser" by Beck and "Mr. Jones" by Counting Crows put the alternative stamp on the year early—Beck reaching number one, and Counting Crows virtually doing the same. Although "Mr. Jones" was never released as a single, it continued to get enough Top 40 airplay to qualify it as one of the top ten songs of the year. How's that for having your alternative cake and eating crow too!

But it seemed as soon as any alternative left field entry (like "Mmm Mmm Mmm Mmm" by the Crash Test Dummies) reached the top of the charts, any previous alternative credibility the band may have had was summarily lost. Unless you were Green Day, whose punky laments like "Longview" and "Basket Case" managed to give them simultaneous pop and underground respect. Beyond fashion and friction, the Top 40 offered us some true underground gems, among them the lovely anti-Beatles "Black Hole Sun," by Chris Cornell of Soundgarden; "Far Behind" by Kevin Martin of Candlebox, about the loss of a friend to drugs; Offspring's comment on racial tension, "Come Out and Play"; Live's treatise on modern living, "Selling the Drama"; and rocker Melissa Etheridge's commercial coming-out party, "Come to My Window" and "I'm the Only One." Classic Alternative, as a form and a format, lent us vintage newies from REM ("What's the Frequency, Kenneth"), the Pretenders ("I'll Stand by You"), and Tom Petty ("You Don't Know How It Feels").

R&B and Rap: Racy, Sexy, Romantic

As welcome and overpublicized as the arrival on the charts of alternative rock and roll was, the preponderance of mainstream success still went to the dance and R&B ditties which had held sway all decade. Though gangsta rap continued in decline, the R&B mixture of sex and innuendo, tied to a steady beat, generally accounted for more than half the tunes on the Top 40 each week. But as opposed to the last few years, powerful moments in this genre were distinctly in the minority. Seal's "Prayer for the Dying" was poignant and unsparing; Des'Ree's enticing "You Gotta Be" was proud and uplifting; US3's "Cantaloop (Flip Fantasia)" creatively welded a Herbie Hancock jazz classic onto a rap setting; and Salt-N-Pepa's "Whatta Man" was a model role model.

More often, however, racy innuendo ruled. The instant smash by 20 Fingers' entitled "Short Short Man" was originally known as "Short Dick Man." There was the unforgettable "Tootsee Roll" by 69 Boys, and "Dunkie Butt" by 12 Gauge. Then there was R. Kelly's one-man assault on decency: his own "Bump and Grind" was followed by "Your Body's Calling." He wrote and produced the insinuating sex fantasy "Stroke You Up" for Changing Faces. Finally, he not only wrote and produced "Back and Forth" for the teenage sex bomb Aaliyah, but wound up running off and marrying her later in the year. As something of an alternative, Crystal Waters' vision of "100% Pure Love" was a woman who was free to roam among several lovers. Summing up such rampant lewdness was left to the earthy trio of Salt-N-Pepa, who told all narrow-minded puritanical censors and right wingers it was "None of Your Business."

Popular Music in 1994

If sex reigned supreme in the world of Top 40 (virtually identical to the world of R&B), its opposite member, romance, also had a banner year. This essential yin and yang (as opposed to "Bump and Grind" and "Back and Forth") was typified by a one-man symbol of yin and yang himself, who has, in the course of his career, gone from nymph to satyr, from name to symbol, and back again. The artist once and undoubtedly once again known as Prince gave us perhaps his most utterly romantic tune, "The Most Beautiful Girl in the World," which debuted during a beauty pageant. All-4-One harmonized sweetly on the old Romantics hit, "So Much in Love," and topped it with "I Swear," which doubled as a country hit for John Michael Montgomery. Then there was the neo-do wop of Boyz II Men with the most gentlemanly "I'll Make Love to You," followed up by the similarly chivalrous "On Bended Knee," occupying the top of the Top 40 as if it were their own boudoir.

The author of the aforementioned tune, Babyface, otherwise known as Kenny Edmunds, also had a romantic year—on his own, with "When Can I See You," and in tandem with Darryl Simmons for himself ("And Our Feelings"), Tevin Campbell ("Always in My Heart," "I'm Ready"), and Aretha Franklin ("Willing to Forgive"). With Simmons and L. A. Reid, Babyface scripted the gorgeous "You Mean the World to Me," for this year's reigning pop soul diva, Toni Braxton. Last year's pop soul princess, Janet Jackson, with co-writers James Harris III and Terry Lewis, didn't do too badly in the romance department (or the hit department) either, with "Because of Love," "Anytime Anyplace/And On and On," and "You Want This."

Neither romantic nor particularly sexy, rap's message was decidedly muted in 1994. The mellowing of gansta rap continued, with Nate Dogg and Warren G's pictorial street scene "Regulate," a direct descendant of Nate's cousin Snoop Doggy Dogg's "Gin and Juice." Ice Cube, with the aid of George Clinton's "One Nation under a Groove," gave us the compelling "Bop Gun (One Nation)." Nevertheless, the energy of Craig Mack's "Flava in Ya Ear" and "Funkdafied" by Da Brat were undeniable, as was the nostalgia touted by Ahmad in "Back in the Day."

Elsewhere in the Top 40, the reggae-lite of Swedish sensations Ace of Base held sway ("The Sign," "Don't Turn Around," "Living in Danger"). More authentic reggae bolted to the top as well, with Ini Kamozi's tongue in chic rap "Here Comes the Hotstepper," from the soundtrack of the movie *Pret-a-Porter (Ready to Wear)*. Classic dance diva and apprentice raconteur Madonna spent much of the year in the top ten, with "Take a Bow" and the earlier "Secret," co-written with Dallas Austin, who also wrote "Creep" for TLC. As usual, there was a place at the top for the pop ballad. Billy Joel's poignant "Lullabye," Joshua Kaddison's "Beautiful in My Eyes," the Mariah Carey-Luther Vandross remake of "Endless Love," and Bon Jovi's heavily cliched "Always" were the prime exponents of this timeless breed.

Reality Sound-Bites: Four Weddings, Three Lion Kings, and a Funeral

Other ballads bolted straight to the charts after clever placement in feature films. The Troggs' wistful oldie "Love Is All Around," by Wet Wet Wet, came our way from England, courtesy of *Four Weddings and a Funeral.* Lisa Loeb's ineffable "Stay (I Missed You)" survived *Reality Bites* to reach number one as a single, despite the relative obscurity of the movie, the total obscurity of the singer, and the charming ambivalence of the song itself. Bruce Springsteen's "Streets of Philadelphia," which won the Oscar for Best Song in 1993 (as well as a Golden Globe), also won a Grammy in 1994. Less surprisingly, Elton John's collaboration with Tim Rice for the score of *The Lion King,* produced three Oscar nominated songs—"Circle of Life," "Hakuna Matata," and the winner, "Can You Feel the Love Tonight."

FM Radio Reinvented

By year's end, Top 40's co-optation of alternative music began to merely seem like just another programming ploy, giving them a tune or two to break the monotony of yet another song by Aerosmith ("Crazy," "Amazing"), Ace of Base, Mariah Carey, the remixed Four Seasons ("December 1963"), or the almost instantly redundant Sheryl Crow ("All I Wanna Do"). This eventuality led to the full flourishing of the alternative format on the radio, a virtual underground network, complete with deep and massive playlists of previously unheralded bands. In effect, a reinvention of FM radio.

While the Dylan and the Beatles of this new revolution continued to be Pearl Jam ("Spin the Black Circle," "Dissident," "Daughter") and Nirvana (an unplugged "Where Did You Sleep Last Night"), 1994's Led Zeppelin would have to be the Stone Temple Pilots, who, while roundly reviled by purists, still somehow managed to lead all the popularity polls ("Vasoline," "Big Empty," "Interstate Love Song").

Morrissey, previously a staple of the format, when it was restricted to the vast legions of effete English mopers and whining boys, was not entirely excluded from the new order ("The More You Ignore Me, the Closer I Get"). Yet, if third world music was conspicuous by its absense, the third sex had only a slighly easier time of reclaiming lost airtime. Now American-made roots rock and rage predominated, led by extravagantly pedigreed '80s survivors like Henry Rollins, once of Black Flag ("Liar"), Cracker's David Lowery, formerly of Camper Van Beethoven ("Low"), and Sugar, headed by Hüsker Dü's Bob Mould ("Your Favorite Thing"). Following 1993's breakthrough acts—Soul Asylum and Paul Westerberg, late of the Replacements—the Meat Puppets ("Backwater") have years of underground credibility. Glenn Danzig's Morrisonesque "Mother" had itself been around for five years. Inspiration for all was provided by Chrissie Hynde's best work in years ("Hollywood Perfume") and the ageless Neil Young's tribute to Kurt Cobain ("Sleeps with Angels").

As well as the inevitable, implicit nods to Cobain, this year's alternative bands also paid tribute to a wide variety of sources, from Tom Petty ("Even the Losers" by Nectarine, "American Girl" by Everclear) and Kiss ("Rock and Roll All Night" by Toad the Wet Sprocket), to Neil Diamond ("Girl You'll Be a Woman Soon" by Urge Overkill) and Stevie Nicks ("Landslide" by Smashing Pumpkins), culminating in a psychic group hug to none other than the Carpenters ("Superstar" by Sonic Youth, "Yesterday Once More" by Redd Kross).

In general, the stylized dancehall drag of previous post modern music gave way to a refreshing punkish amateurishness, and a return to lyrics with bite and meaning. There was "Zombie" by the Cranberries, about the troubles in Northern Ireland; the terrifying glance into love's deeper recesses, "Closer" by Trent Reznor of Nine Inch Nails; "No Excuses" by Jerry Cantrell of Alice in Chains; and "Spoonman" by Chris Cornell of Soundgarden. Pearl Jam's "Better Man" quickly established itself as a monster. With tunes like "Seether," "What Jail Is Like," and "21st Century (Digital Boy)," Veruca Salt, the Afghan Whigs, and Bad Religion established themselves as monsters of the future. Tori Amos ("God") crawled another couple of inches toward the hem of Kate Bush's sacred garment. Liz Phair ("Supernova") and Cobain's widow Courtney Love ("Miss World") spoke the female language with rock and roll bluntness, causing other alternative rockers to make fun ("New Age Girl" by Deadeye Dick) or otherwise retreat ("Buddy Holly" by Weezer). Even without the calculating fanfare of a Woodstock II to announce their arrival into prominence, the individual and collective talent of the new underground would have been enough to ensure their survival.

Page and Plant Lead Rock Stalwarts

Which of them will survive for twenty years or more is another wager. For even as classic rock took the biggest hit to the body and the mind this year, as far as general relevance and good music, its few returning veterans and reunited heroes were as hardy a lot as ever. Jimmy Page and Robert Plant hardly looked a day over forty as they graced the covers of the rock press prior to their near-Zeppelin redux world tour ("Gallows Pole"). Covered with moss and sawdust and assorted wrinkles, the Rolling Stones nevertheless commanded the entire music section of a national entertainment magazine when their latest album and tour arrived ("You Got Me Rocking"). Pink Floyd seems well situated for the millenium ("Keep Talking"). Neil Young was as feisty as ever ("Piece of Crap") and Joni Mitchell as cantankerous ("Love Kilis"). Walter Becker rejoined his former other half, Donald Fagen, for a Steely Dan tour and a new solo album ("Down in the Bottom"). Bob Dylan put out another set of greatest hits with consummate "Dignity." Though comparative youngsters, John Mellencamp ("Dance Naked," "Wild Nights"), had to cancel a tour midway through due to illness, as did Don Henley and Glenn Frey of the resurgent Eagles ("Get Over It").

Country Searches for Roots, AAA Remains in Obscurity

Many in the classic rock constituency, being well above the age of consent, finally neared and passed the age when the safe familiar rhythms of country music began to appeal to them more than the relative cacophony of everything else. Yet, in country music itself, most of this year's few redeeming moments came when downhome musicians tapped into those selfsame outside genres for some much needed energy and inspiration.

One of the chief beneficiaries of this search for roots was the Eagles ("Desperado" by Clint Black, "Take It Easy" by Randy Travis). Another side of Garth Brooks was revealed when he covered the Kiss classic "Hard Luck Woman." The country/R&B tribute/collaboration went back a little deeper, and was a vivid aural reminder of the days when both forms were fighting for the soul of rock and roll ("Something Else," the Eddie Cochran-Sharon Sheeley standard, reinterpreted by Little Richard and Tanya Tucker, and Brook Benton's "Rainy Night in Georgia," redone by Sam Moore and Conway Twitty). Even uptown in commercial country, this quest for roots took hold (Alan Jackson's revival of "Summertime Blues" and Faith Hill's remake of Janis Joplin's "Piece of My Heart").

For the most part, the fern bar of suburban yuppiehood predominated country music's reluctance to tamper with a winning formula. Breaking from the mold was difficult, but, as proven by Martina McBride ("Independence Day") or Kathy Mattea ("Walking Away a Winner") or Vince Gill ("Where Love Finds You"), not impossible. On the other hand, as evidenced by Billy Ray Cyrus' achy-breakthrough in 1992, bad taste ("Indian Outlaw" by Tim McGraw) is timeless.

If the wheel of the underground pointed to punk in 1994, those artsy denizens of the Adult Album Alternative (AAA) format were content to produce and develop in relative obscurity for another year. The folk/rock of the '90s welcomed even more escapees from the other formats this year, listeners and artists alike, who appreciate more than image, more than revolution, but a good song above all.

In this context, the reigning poet laureate was clearly Richard Thompson, the recipient of a tribute album ("I Misunderstood" by Dinosaur Jr.), a nod from the Queen Mother ("Dimming of the Day" covered by Bonnie Raitt), and another solo gem of a release ("Beeswing"). The crown prince of verbiage, Elvis Costello, lived up to his legend ("Thirteen Steps Lead Down," "Just About Glad"). Mary Chapin Carpenter mourned the legacy of folk/rock's last great moment in "Stones in the Road." Joni Mitchell stood up for it in "Vyette in English." Format veterans Lyle Lovett ("Creeps Like Us"), Nancy Griffith ("Time of Inconvenience"), John Gorka ("Thoughtless Behavior"), and Cheryl Wheeler ("When Fall Comes to New England") were joined by the new literati, Victoria Williams ("Crazy Mary"), Iris Dement ("No Time to Cry"), the Indigo Girls ("The Power of Two"), Ben Harper ("I'll Rise"), and Freedy Johnston ("Bad Reputation").

Promoted by no less a surprising benefactor than MTV, pure poetry stepped center stage for a while in 1994, unplugged and unhyped ("A Prayer" by Lisa Buscani, "Please Don't Take My Air Jordans" by Reg E. Gaines). Never ones to let an opportunity to hip the intelligensia to the real thing, Rhino records released Allen Ginsberg's *Holy Soul Jelly Roll: Songs and Poems 1948–1993*, which contained the poem "Howl," the seminal beatnik epic from which arguably all of folk/rock subsequently sprung.

To those for whom no alternative is prudent or necessary, the only drama offered each year by the musical theater is whether there will be enough shows on or off Broadway to provide sufficient nominees for the annual Obie and Tony awards. By these standards of feast or famine, 1994 was a definite feast. There was the new *Passion* from Sondheim ("Loving You"), the new *Sunset Boulevard* remake from Lloyd Webber ("As If We Never Said Goodbye"), and the newly refurbished *A Doll's House* by Betty Comden and Adolph Green ("There She Is"). Michael John LaChuisa's *Hello Again* ("Hello Again") was a tour de force. Composer Alan Menken accounted for a double feature, the Disneyized *Beauty & the Beast* ("If I Can't Love Her") and the updated *Scrooge* ("Christmas Together"). The country music musical *Chippie* accounted for a triple play, with tunes by Butch Hancock ("Low Lights of Town"), Joe Ely ("Whiskey and Woman and Money to Burn"), and Jo Carol Pierce ("Across the Great Divide") long outlasting the play itself. Other quick exits were experienced by Carol Hall's *Best Little Whorehouse Goes Public* ("I'm Leaving Texas") and Yoko Ono's *New York Rock* ("Yes, I'm Your Angel"). But subtle pleasures were to be derived from Polly Pen's *Christina Alberta's Father* ("Uneasy Armchairs") and *Inside Out* by Russ Adryan and Doug Haverty ("No One Inside"). By far the year's most innovative, you might say alternative, use of theatre music emanated from well off Broadway, down on New York's lower East Side, where bands named Uncle Wiggly, the Lunachicks, Iron Prostate, and others, got together for an amazingly condensed rendering of the Peter Townshend magnum opus, appropriately retitled for the occasion, "Tommy in Seven Minutes."

Bruce Pollock
Editor

A

About a Girl
Words and music by Kurt Cobain.
EMI-Virgin, 1990/End of Music, 1990.
Introduced by Nirvana on *MTV Unplugged in New York* (DGC, 94).

Across the Great Divide
Words and music by Jo Carol Pierce.
Lucky Nakedress, Austin, 1994.
Introduced by Jo Carol Pierce in the musical and on the cast album
  Chippie (Hollywood, 94).

All Apologies
Words and music by Kurt Cobain.
EMI-Virgin, 1992/End of Music, 1992.
Best-selling record by Nirvana from *In Utero* (DOC/Gelfen, 93). After
  his death, Kurt Cobain attained legendary status as spokesman of a
  teen generation. Nominated for a Grammy Award, Best Rock Song of
  the Year, 1994.

All I Wanna Do
Words and music by Sheryl Crow, Bill Bottrell, David Baerwald, Kevin
  Gilbert, and Wyn Cooper.
Old Crow, Los Angeles, 1994/WB Music, 1994/Warner-Tamerlane
  Music, 1994/Ignorant, 1994/Zen of Iniquity, 1994/Dave Mason Music,
  1994/Canvas Mattress, 1994/Almo/Irving, 1994.
Best-selling record by Sheryl Crow from *Tuesday Night Music Club* (A
  & M, 94). Won a Grammy Award for Best Record of the Year 1994.
  Nominated for a Grammy Award, Best Song of the Year, 1994.

Allison Road
Words and music by Robin Wilson.
WB Music, 1992/East Jesus, 1992.
Introduced by Gin Blossoms on *New Miserable Experience* (A & M,
  93).

1

Almost
Words and music by Cheryl Wheeler.
Amachrist Music, 1994/Penrod & Higgins, 1994.
Introduced by Cheryl Wheeler on *Driving Home* (Philo, 94).

Always
Words and music by Jon Bon Jovi.
Polygram International, 1994/Bon Jovi Publishing, 1994.
Best-selling record by Bon Jovi from *Cross Roads* (Mercury, 94).

Always (English)
Words and music by Vince Clarke and Andy Bell.
Sony Music, 1994/Musical Moments, 1994/Minotaur, 1994.
Best-selling record by Erasure from the album *I Say, I Say, I Say* (Mute/ Elektra, 94).

Always in My Heart
Words and music by Babyface (pseudonym for Kenny Edmunds) and Daryl Simmons.
Sony Songs, 1994/Ecaf, 1994/Boobie-Loo, 1994/Warner-Tamerlane Music, 1994.
Best-selling record by Tevin Campbell from the album *I'm Ready* (Quest/Warner Bros., 94).

Am I Wrong (English)
Words and music by Tom Butler and Richard Butler.
Wedding Song, 1994/Irving Music Inc., 1994/Fail Safe, 1994.
Introduced by Love Spit Love on *Love Spit Love* (Imago, 94).

Amazing
Words and music by Steven Tyler and Richard Supa.
Swag Song Music, 1993/Alien Music, 1993/Super Supa Songs, 1993.
Best-selling record by Aerosmith from *Get a Grip* (Geffen, 93).

American Girl
Words and music by Tom Petty.
Almo Music Corp., 1977.
Revived by Tom Petty and the Heartbreakers on *Greatest Hits* (MCA, 94). Also, released by Everclear on *Get Lucky* (Backyard/Scotti Bros., 94).

And Our Feelings
Words and music by Babyface (pseudonym for Kenny Edmunds) and Daryl Simmons.
Sony Songs, 1994/Ecaf, 1994/Boobie-Loo, 1994/Warner-Tamerlane Music, 1994.
Best-selling record by Babyface from *For the Cool in You* (Epic, 93).

Andres
Words and music by Suzi Gardner and Donita Sparks.
Drop Trou Tunes, New York, 1994.
Introduced by L7 on *Hungry for Stink* (Slash, 94).

Anna
Words and music by Arthur Alexander.
Painted Desert Music Corp., 1962/Keva Music Co., 1962.
Revived by Roger McGuinn on *Adios Amigo: A Tribute to Arthur Alexander* (Razor & Tie, 94). Vintage R&B tune once covered by the Beatles.

Another Night (German)
English words and music by J. Winding, O. Quickmix, and Jeglitza.
Copyright Control, 1994.
Introduced by Real McCoy (Arista, 94).

Anything
Words and music by Bryan Alexander Morgan.
Warner-Tamerlane Music, 1993/Interscope Pearl, 1993/Bam Jams, 1993.
Best-selling record by SWV in the film and on the soundtrack *Above the Rim* (RCA, 94).

Anytime, Any Place/And On and On
Words and music by Janet Jackson, James Harris, III, and Terry Lewis.
Black Ice Music, 1994/Flyte Tyme Tunes, 1994.
Best-selling record by Janet Jackson from the album *janet* (Virgin, 94).

Anytime You Need a Friend
Words and music by Mariah Carey and Walter Afanasieff.
Sony Songs, 1994/Rye Songs, 1994/WB Music, 1994/Wally World, 1994.
Best-selling record by Mariah Carey from the album *Music Box* (Columbia, 94).

As If We Never Said Goodbye
Music by Andrew Lloyd Webber, words by Don Black and Christopher Hampton.
Music by Candlelight, 1993/PSO Ltd., 1993.
Introduced by Glenn Close on the musical and Broadway cast album *Sunset Boulevard* (A & M, 94).

At Your Best (You Are Love)
Words and music by Ernie Isley, Marvin Isley, O'Kelly Isley, Ronald Isley, Rudolph Isley, and Chris Jasper.
Bovina Music, Inc., 1976/EMI-April Music, 1976.
Revived by Aaliyah from *Age Ain't Nothin' but a Number* (Blackground/Jive, 94).

3

B

Baby I Can't Please You
Words and music by Sam Phillips.
Eden Bridge Music, 1994.
Introduced by Sam Phillips on *Martinis and Bikinis* (Virgin, 94).

Baby I Love Your Way
Words and music by Peter Frampton.
Almo Music Corp., 1976/Nuages Artists Music Ltd., 1976.
Revived by Big Mountain in the film and on the soundtrack album
    Reality Bites (RCA, 94).

Back & Forth
Words and music by Robert Kelly.
Zomba Music, 1994/R. Kelly Music, 1994.
Best-selling record by Aaliyah from the album *Age Ain't Nothin' but a
    Number* (Blackground, 94).

Back in the Box
Words and music by David Byrne.
Moldy Pig, 1994.
Introduced by David Byrne on *David Byrne* (Luaka Bop, 94).

Back in the Day
Words and music by Ahmad Lewis and Stefan Gordy.
Ahmad, 1994/WB Music, 1994/Kendall, 1994.
Best-selling record by Ahmad from the album *Ahmad* (Giant, 94).

Back Where It All Begins
Words and music by Richard Belts.
Pangola, 1994/EMI-Blackwood Music Inc., 1994.
Introduced by The Allman Brothers on *Back Where It All Begins* (Epic,
    94).

Backwater
Words and music by Curt Kirkwood.
Songs of Polygram, 1994/Meat Puppets, 1994.

Best-selling record by Meat Puppets from *Too High to Die* (Londen, 94).

Bad Reputation
Words and music by Freedy Johnston.
Rock City Crackers, 1994/EMI-Blackwood Music Inc., 1994.
Introduced by Freedy Johnston on *Perfect World* (Elektra, 94).

Baltimore
Words and music by Tom Meltzer.
Rock City Crackers, 1991/Songs of Polygram, 1991.
Revived by Five Chinese Brothers on *Rig Rock Jukebox* (Diesel Only, 94).

Bannerman
Words and music by Steve Taylor.
Warner Alliance, 1993/Soylent Tunes, 1993.
Introduced by Steve Taylor on *Squint* (Warner Alliance, 94).

Basket Case
Words by Billy Joe.
Warner-Chappell Music, 1994.
Best-selling record by Green Day from the album *Dookie* (Reprise, 94).

Be Happy
Words by Mary J. Blige and Arlene Delvalle, music by Sean Combs and Jean Oliver.
MCA Music, 1994/Mary J. Blige, 1994/Dooch, 1994/Twelve & Under, 1994/EMI-April Music, 1994/Justin Publishing Co., 1994.
Best-selling record by Mary J. Blige from *My Life* (RCA, 94).

Be My Baby Tonight
Words and music by Ed Hill and Rich Fagan.
Music Hill, Nashville, 1994/New Haven, 1994/Of, 1994.
Best-selling record by John Michael Montgomery from the album *Kickin' It Up* (Atlantic, 94).

Be Our Guest
Music by Alan Menken, words by Tim Rice.
Walt Disney Music, 1991/Wonderland Music, 1991.
Introduced by the castle staff in *Beauty and the Beast*.

Beautiful in My Eyes
Words and music by Joshua Kadison.
Joshuasongs, 1993/Seymour Glass, 1993/EMI-Blackwood Music Inc., 1993.
Best-selling record by Joshua Kadison from *Painted Desert Serenade* (SBK/ERG, 93).

6

Because of Love
Words and music by Janet Jackson, James Harris, III, and Terry Lewis.
Black Ice Music, 1994/Flyte Tyme Tunes, 1994.
Best-selling record by Janet Jackson from *janet* (Virgin, 93).

Before I Let You Go
Words and music by Teddy Riley, Leon Sylvers, Melvin Riley,
  Chauncey Hannibal, and Dave Hollister.
Donril Music, 1994/Zomba Music, 1994/MCA Music, 1994/Tadej, 1994/
  Davey Pooh, 1994/Chauncey Black, 1994.
Best-selling record by Blackstreet from *Blackstreet* (Interscope, 94).

Before You Kill Us All
Words and music by Keith Follese and Max D. Barnes.
Careers-BMG, 1994/Famous Music Corp., 1994/Island Bound, 1994/
  Breaker Maker, 1994.
Best-selling record by Randy Travis from the album *This Is Me* (Warner
  Bros., 94).

Big Empty
Words and music by Dean DeLeo and Scott Weiland.
EMI-10, 1994/Floated Music, 1994/Pressmancherry, 1994/WB Music,
  1994.
Best-selling record by Stone Temple Pilots from the film and soundtrack
  album *The Crow* (Atlantic/Interscope, 94).

The Big One
Words and music by Gerry House and Devon O'Day.
Housenotes, Hermitage, 1994.
Best-selling record by George Strait from *Lead On* (MCA, 94).

Big Yellow Taxi
Words and music by Joni Mitchell.
Siquomb Publishing Corp., 1970.
Revived by Maire Brennan on *Misty Eyed Adventure* (Atlantic, 94).

Birdbrain
Words and music by Allen Ginsberg.
Introduced by Allen Ginsberg on *Holy Soul Jelly Roll: Songs and
  Poems 1948-1993* (Atlantic, 94).

Bizarre Love Triangle (English)
Words and music by Bernard Dickins, Gillian Gilbert, Peter Hooh, and
  Stephen Morris.
WB Music, 1986.
Revived by Frente! from *Marvin the Album* (Mammouth, 94).

Black Hole Sun
Words and music by Chris Cornell.

7

You Make Me Sick, I Make Music, 1994.
Best-selling record Soundgarden *Superunknown* (A & M, 94). Anti-Beatles lament established new hard rock standard. Nominated for a Grammy Award, Best Rock Song of the Year, 1994.

Blackbird (English)
Words and music by Paul McCartney and John Lennon.
Northern Music Corp., 1969/Maclen Music Inc., 1969.
Revived by Dionne Farris on *Wild Seed-Wild Flower* (Columbia, 94).

Blind Man
Words and music by Steven Tyler, Joe Perry, and Taylor Rhodes.
Swag Song Music, 1994/EMI-April Music, 1994/MCA Music, 1994/Taylor Rhodes Music, 1994.
Introduced by Aerosmith on *Big Ones* (Geffen, 94).

Bob George
Words and music by Prince.
Controversy Music, 1987.
Revived by Prince on *The Black Album* (Warner Bros., 94). Long suppressed bootleg album finally sees the light.

Body & Soul
Words and music by Ellen Shipley and Rick Nowels.
EMI-Virgin, 1994/Shipwreck, 1994/EMI Music Publishing, 1994/Future Furniture, 1994.
Best-selling record by Anita Baker from *Rhythm of Love* (Elektra, 94). Nominated for a Grammy Award, Best Rhythm 'n Blues Song of the Year, 1994.

Booti Call
Words and music by Teddy Riley, Erick Sermon, Leon Sylvers, Melvin Riley, Antwone Dickey, and Roger Troutman.
Donril Music, 1994/Zomba Music, 1994/Ludlow Music Inc., 1994/Tadej, 1994/Color It Funky, 1994/Erick Sermon, 1994/Saja Music Co., 1994/Troutman's, 1994.
Best-selling record by Blackstreet from the album *Blacksteet* (Interscope, 94).

Bop Gun (One Nation)
Words and music by Ice Cube, George Clinton, Jr., Gary Shider, Walter Morrison, and Q. D. III.
Gangsta Boogie, 1994/WB Music, 1994/Deep Technology, 1994/Full Keel Music, 1994.
Best-selling record by Ice Cube featuring George Clinton from *Lethal Injection* (Priority, 94). This song updates the Funkadelic classic *One Nation Under a Groove*.

Born to Roll
Words and music by Duvall Clear.
Damasta, 1993/Varry White Music, 1993.
Best-selling record by Masta Ace Incorporated from *Slaughtahouse* (Delicious Vinyl, 93).

Breathe Again
Words and music by Ed Roland.
Roland/Lentz, New York, 1994.
Best-selling record by Collective Soul from *Hints, Allegations & Things Left Unsaid* (Atlantic, 94).

Buddy Holly
Words and music by Rivers Cuomo.
E. O. Smith, West Los Angeles, 1994.
Best-selling record by Weezer on *Weezer* (DGC, 94).

Bump and Grind
Words and music by Robert Kelly.
Zomba Music, 1993/R. Kelly Music, 1993.
Best-selling record by R. Kelly from *12 Play* (Jive, 93).

C

Callin' Baton Rouge
Words and music by Dennis Linde.
Columbine Music Inc., 1994/EMI-Blackwood Music Inc., 1994.
Best-selling record by Garth Brooks from *In Pieces* (Liberty, 93).

Can You Feel the Love Tonight (English)
Music by Elton John, words by Tim Rice.
Walt Disney Music, 1994.
Best-selling record by Elton John from the film and soundtrack album
    The Lion King (Hollywood, 94). Won an Academy Award for Best
    Original Song of the Year 1994. Nominated for Grammy Awards,
    Best Movie or TV Song of the Year, 1994 and Best Song of the
    Year, 1994.

Can't You Hear I'm Making Love to You
Music by Larry Grossman, words by Betty Comden and Adolph Green.
Revelation Music Publishing Corp., 1994/Betdolph Music, 1994/Manor
    Lane, 1994/Fiddleback, 1994.
Introduced by Jill Geddes and Tom Galantech in *A Doll's Life*.

Cantaloop (Flip Fantasia)
Music by Herbie Hancock, words and music by Geoff Wilkinson and
    Mel Simpson.
EMI-Blackwood Music Inc., 1993/US3, 1993.
Best-selling record by US3 from *Hand on the Torch* (Blue Note/Capitol,
    93).

Change in Me
Words and music by Carole Hall.
Introduced by Scott Holmes in *The Best Little Whorehouse Goes Public*.

Change Your Mind
Words and music by Neil Young.
Silver Fiddle, 1994.

Introduced by Neil Young and Crazy Horse on *Sleeps with Angels* (Reprise, 94).

Chaos and Void
Words and music by Peter Himmelman.
Himmasongs, 1993.
Introduced by Peter Himmelman on *Skin* (550 Music/Epic, 94).

Children of the Future
Words and music by Mose Allison.
Audre Mae Music, 1994.
Introduced by Mose Allison on *The Earth Wants You* (Blue Note, 94).

Choose
Words and music by James Harris, III and Terry Lewis.
Flyte Tyme Tunes, 1993/Me Good Music, 1993.
Best-selling record by Color Me Badd from *Time and Change* (Giant/ Reprise, 93).

Christmas Together
Music by Alan Menken, words by Lynn Ahrens.
Introduced by the cast of *A Christmas Carol*.

Circle Dance
Words and music by Bonnie Raitt.
Open Secret, Los Angeles, 1993.
Introduced by Bonnie Raitt on *Longing in Their Hearts* (Capitol, 94).

Circle of Life (English)
Music by Elton John, words by Tim Rice.
Wonderland Music, 1993.
Best-selling record by Elton John from the film and soundtrack *The Lion King* (Walt Disney Records, 94). Nominated for an Academy Award, Best Original Song of the Year, 1994; Nominated for an Academy Award, Best Original Song of the Year, 1994; Grammy Awards, Best Movie or TV Song of the Year, 1994 and Best Song of the Year, 1994.

Closer to Free
Words and music by Sammy Llanas and Kurt Neumann.
Lla-Mann, 1994.
Introduced by The Bodeans on *Go Down Slow* (Slash, 94).

Come Out and Play
Words and music by Dexter Holland, Greg K., Noodles, and Ron Welty.
Gamete, Huntington Beach, 1994.
Best-selling record by Offspring from *Smash* (Epitaph, 94). Treatise on gang relations.

Come to My Window
Words and music by Melissa Etheridge.
MLE Music, 1994/Alamo Music, Inc., 1994.
Introduced by Melissa Etheridge on *Yes I Am* (Island, 93). Nominated
   for a Grammy Award, Best Rock Song of the Year, 1994.

Completely
Words and music by Diane Warren.
Realsongs, 1993.
Best-selling record by Michael Bolton from *The One Thing* (Columbia,
   93).

Constantly
Words and music by Ian Prince, D. Pearson, Jesse Powell, and Teron
   Beal.
EMI-April Music, 1994/EMI Music Publishing, 1994/Jesse Powell,
   1994/Teron Beal, 1994.
Best-selling record by Immature from *Playtyme Is Over* (MCA, 94).

Cornflake Girl (English)
Words and music by Tori Amos.
Sword and Stone, 1994.
Introduced by Tori Amos on *Under the Pink* (Atlantic, 94). This is
   Amos's first single in the U.K.

Crazy
Words and music by Steven Tyler, Joe Perry, and Desmond Child.
Swag Song Music, 1994/EMI-April Music, 1994/Desmobile Music Inc.,
   1994.
Best-selling record by Aerosmith from the album *Get a Grip* (Geffen,
   94).

Crazy
Words and music by Willie Nelson.
Tree Publishing Co., Inc., 1961.
Revived by Willie Nelson and Jimmie Dale Gilmore on *Red, Hot and
   Country* (Mercury, 94).

Crazy Mary
Words and music by Victoria Williams.
Mumblety Peg, 1993/Careers-BMG, 1993.
Revived by Victoria Williams on *Loose* (Atlantic, 94).

Creep
Words and music by Dallas Austin.
EMI-April Music, 1994/D.A.R.P. Music, 1994.
Best-selling record by TLC from *Crazy Sexy Cool* (LaFace, 94).

Creeps Like Me
Words and music by Lyle Lovett.
Michael H. Goldsen, Inc., 1994.
Introduced by Lyle Lovett on *I Love Everybody* (Curb, 94).

Cuban Pete
Words and music by Jose Norman (pseudonym for Norman Henderson).
Sam Fox, Santa Barbara, 1936/Edward Kassner Music, New York, 1936.
Revived in 1994 by Jim Carrey in the film and on the soundtrack album
   of *The Mask* (Chaos, 94).

D

Dance Naked
Words and music by John Mellencamp.
Full Keel Music, 1994.
Introduced by John Mellencamp on *Dance Naked* (Mercury, 94).

Dark End of the Street
Words and music by Chips Moman and Dan Penn.
EMI Music Publishing, 1967.
Revived by Dan Penn on *Do Right Man* (Sire, 94).

Daughter
Music by Dave Abbruzzese, Jeff Ament, Stone Gossard, and Mike
    McCready, words and music by Eddie Vedder.
Innocent Bystander Music, 1993/Write Treatage Music, 1993/Scribing
    C-Ment Music, 1993/Jumping Cat Music, 1993.
Best-selling record by Pearl Jam from *Vs* (Epic, 93).

December 1963 (Oh, What a Night)
Words and music by Bob Gaudio and Judy Parker.
Seasons Music Co., 1975/Jobete Music Co., 1975.
Revived by The Four Seasons (Curb, 94). The remix sparked remarkable
    resurgence of the retired record.

A Deeper Love
Words and music by David Cole and Rob Clivilles.
EMI-Virgin, 1992/Cole-Clivilles Music, 1992.
Introduced by Aretha Franklin in the film and on the soundtrack *Sister
    Act 2* (Arista, 93).

Desperado
Words and music by Don Henley and Glenn Frey.
Cass County Music Co., 1973/Red Cloud Music Co., 1973.
Revived by Clint Black on *Common Threads: The Songs of the Eagles*
    (Grant, 94). This country tribute to the group the Eagles soared in the
    rankings.

Deuces Are Wild
Words and music by Steven Tyler and Joe Perry.
Swag Song Music, 1993/EMI-April Music, 1993.
Best-selling record by Aerosmith on *The Beavis and Butthead Experience* (Geffen, 93).

Dignity
Words and music by Bob Dylan.
Special Rider Music, 1994.
Introduced by Bob Dylan on *Bob Dylan's Greatest Hits* (Columbia, 94).

Dimming of the Day
Words and music by Richard Thompson.
Songs of Polygram, 1993.
Revived by Bonnie Raitt on *Longing in Their Hearts* (Capitol, 94).

Dirty Dawg
Words and music by Donnie Wahlberg, L. Thomas, J. Jackson, and J. Johnson.
WB Music, 1994/Donnie D., 1994/Jordan Knight, 1994/Nice & Smooth, 1994.
Best-selling record by NKOTB on *Face the Music* (Columbia, 94).

Dissident
Music by Dave Abbruzzese, Jeff Ament, Stone Gossard, and Mike McCready, words and music by Eddie Vedder.
Innocent Bystander Music, 1993/Write Treatage Music, 1993/Scribing C-Ment Music, 1993/Jumping Cat Music, 1993.
Best-selling record by Pearl Jam on *Vs* (Epic, 93).

Do You Wanna Get Funky
Words and music by Rob Clivilles, David Cole, and Duran Ramos.
Cole-Clivilles Music, 1994/Duranman, 1994/EMI-Virgin, 1994.
Introduced by C + C Music Factory from *Anything Goes* (Columbia, 94).

Don't Take the Girl
Words and music by Craig Martin and Larry Johnson.
Eric Zanetis, Nashville, 1994.
Best-selling record by Tim McGraw from *Not a Moment Too Soon* (Curb, 1994).

Don't Turn Around (Swedish)
English words and music by Albert Hammond and Diane Warren.
Albert Hammond Enterprises, 1991/WB Music, 1991/Realsongs, 1991/ Edition Sunset Publishing Inc., 1991/BMG Music, 1991.
Best-selling record by Ace of Base from *The Sign* (Arista, 94).

Down in the Bottom
Words and music by Walter Becker.
MCA Music, 1994.
Introduced by Walter Becker in *11 Tracks of Whacks*.

Down on the Farm
Words and music by Kerry Kurt Phillips and Jerry Laseter.
Texas Wedge, 1994/Noosa Heads, 1994.
Best-selling record by Tim McGraw from *Not a Moment Too Soon*
  (Curb, 94).

Dreaming with My Eyes Open
Words and music by Tony Arata.
Famous Music Corp., 1994/Pookie Bear, 1994/Bug Music, 1994.
Best-selling record by Clay Walker from the album *Clay Walker* (Giant,
  94).

Dreams (Irish)
Words and music by Noel Hogan and Dolores O'Riordan.
Polygram International, 1993.
Best-selling record by The Cranberries from *Everybody Else Is Doing It,
  So Why Can't We?* (Island, 93).

Dunkie Butt (Please, Please, Please)
Words and music by Ian Pinkney and Robert Gordon.
AMI, Los Angeles, 1994.
Best-selling record by 12 Gauge from *12 Gauge* (Street Life, 94). The
  James Brown refrain is tied to a lyric about rears.

E

Easy's Getting Harder Every Day
Words and music by Iris DeMent.
Songs of Iris, 1993.
Introduced by Iris DeMent on *My Life* (Warner Bros., 94).

Einstein on the Beach (for an Eggman)
Words and music by Adam Duritz, David Bryson, Charlie Gillingham,
Matt Malloy, and Steve Bowman.
EMI-Blackwood Music Inc., 1994/Jones Fall Music, 1994.
Best-selling record by Counting Crows from the album *DGC Rarities
Vol. 1* (DGC/Geffen, 94).

Elderly Woman behind the Counter
Words and music by Dave Abbruzzese, Jeff Ament, Stone Gossard,
Mike McCready, and Eddie Vedder.
Innocent Bystander Music, 1993/Write Treatage Music, 1993/Scribing
C-Ment Music, 1993/Jumping Cat Music, 1993.
Best-selling record by Pearl Jam from *Vs* (Epic, 93).

Endless Love
Words and music by Lionel Richie.
PGO, 1981/Brockman Music, 1981/Colpix, 1981.
Revived by Luther Vandross & Mariah Carey on *Songs* (Epic, 94).

Even the Losers
Words and music by Tom Petty.
Almo Music Corp., 1979.
Revived by Nectarine on *You Got Lucky* (Backyard/Scotti Brothers, 94).

Ever Fallen in Love (with Someone You Shouldn't've) (English)
Words and music by Pete Shelley.
EMI-Virgin, 1979.
Revived by The Buzzcocks on *Love Bites/Another Music in a Different
Kitchen* (I.R.S., 94). Revival of out-of-print album.

Every Day of the Week
Words and music by Antonia Armato, R. Jerald, and K. Miller.
Ju Ju Be, Marietta, 1994/Irving Music Inc., 1994/Armato, 1994/Little Jerald, 1994.
Best-selling record by Jade from *Mind, Body & Song* (Giant/Warner Bros., 94).

Every Generation Has Its Own Disease (German)
Words and music by Fury in the Slaughterhouse
BMG Music, 1994.
Best-selling record by Fury in the Slaughterhouse from *Mono* (RCA, 94).

Every Once in a While
Words and music by Henry Paul, Vern Stephenson, and Dave Robbins.
EMI-Blackwood Music Inc., 1994/Stroudacaster, 1994/WB Music, 1994.
Best-selling record by BlackHawk from the album *BlackHawk* (Arista, 94).

Everyday (English)
Words and music by Phil Collins.
Philip Collins, Ltd., 1993/Hit & Run Music, 1993/WB Music, 1993.
Best-selling record by Phil Collins from *Both Sides* (Atlantic, 93).

Everywhere I Go
Words and music by Jackson Browne.
Swallow Turn Music, 1993.
Introduced by Jackson Browne on *I'm Alive* (Elektra, 93).

Evie's Tears
Words and music by Freedy Johnston.
Trouble Tree, 1994.
Introduced by Freedy Johnston in *Perfect World* (Elektra, 94).

F

Fa All Y'All
Words and music by Jermaine Dupri and Da Brat.
So So Def Music, 1994/EMI-April Music, 1994/Air Control, 1994.
Best-selling record by Da Brat from *Funkdafied* (So So Def/Chaos, 94).

Fade into You (English)
Words and music by David Roback and Hope Sandoval.
Salley Gardens, New York, 1994.
Best-selling record by Mazzy Star from *So Tonight That I Might See*
    (Capitol, 94).

Fall Down
Words and music by Todd Nichols and Glen Phillips.
Sony Music, 1993/Wet Sprocket Songs, 1993.
Best-selling record by Toad the Wet Sprocket from *Dulcinea* (Columbia,
    94).

Fantastic Voyage
Words and music by Artis Ivey, Brian Dobbs, Fred Alexander, Norman
    Beavers, Marvin Craig, Tiemeyer McCain, and Thomas Oliver
    Shelby.
T-Boy Music Publishing Co., Inc., 1980/Boo Daddy, 1980/Portrait-Solar,
    1980/Circle L Publishing, 1980.
Best-selling record by Coolio from the album *It Takes a Thief* (Tommy
    Boy, 94).

Far Behind
Words and music by Kevin Martin.
Skinny White Butt, 1993/Maverick, 1993/WB Music, 1993.
Best-selling record by Candlebox from *Candlebox* (Maverick/Warner
    Bros., 93). The rock lyric of the year about a friend who died too
    soon.

Fast Food
Words and music by Richard Thompson.

Polygram International, 1994.
Introduced by Richard Thompson on *Mirror Blue* (Capitol, 94).

A Father and Two Sons
Music by Rory Block.
American Bible Society, 1994.
Introduced by Rory Block and Jordan Block Valdina on *Angel of Mercy* (Rounder, 94).

Feel the Pain
Words and music by Joseph Mascis.
Spam As the Breed, 1994/Zomba Music, 1994.
Introduced by Dinosaur Jr. on *Without a Sound* (Sire, 94).

Feenin'
Words and music by DeVante Swing.
EMI-April Music, 1993/Deswing Mob, 1993.
Best-selling record by Jodeci from *Diary of a Mad Band* (Uptown, 93).

Finding Myself Lost Again (Irish)
Words and music by Eleanor McEvoy.
EMI-Blackwood Music Inc., 1993/Blue Dandelion, 1993.
Introduced by Eleanor McEvoy on *Eleanor McEvoy* (Geffen, 93).

Fire on Babylon (Irish)
Words and music by Sinead O'Connor and John Reynolds.
EMI Music Publishing, 1994/EMI-Blackwood Music Inc., 1994.
Introduced by Sinead O'Connor on *Universal Mother* (Ensign/Chrysalis, 94).

5 Minutes Alone
Words and music by Philip Anselmo, Dimebag Darrel, Rex, and Vinnie Paul.
Cota Music, 1994.
Introduced by Pantera on *Far Beyond Driven* (East/West, 94).

Flava in Ya Ear
Words and music by Craig Mack.
For Ya Ear, 1994/Janice Combs, 1994/EMI-April Music, 1994/Bee Mo Easy, 1994.
Best-selling record by Craig Mack from *Project: Funk the World* (Bad Boy/Arista, 94).

Fly like a Bird
Words and music by Boz Scaggs.
Windover Lake Songs, Los Angles, 1993.
Introduced by Boz Scaggs on *Some Change* (Virgin, 94).

Foolish Pride
Words and music by Travis Tritt.
Post Oak, 1994.
Best-selling record by Travis Tritt from the album *Ten Feet Tall and Bulletproof* (Warner Bros., 94).

Found Out about You
Words and music by Doug Hopkins.
WB Music, 1992/East Jesus, 1992.
Best-selling record by the Gin Blossoms from *New Miserable Experience* (A & M, 93).

From a Sympathetical Hurricane
Words and music by Bobby Sichran.
Bombi Beat, 1994/WB Music, 1994.
Introduced by Bobby Sichran on *From a Sympathetical Hurricane* (Columbia, 94).

Funkdafied
Words and music by Jermaine Dupri and Da Brat.
So So Def Music, 1994/EMI-April Music, 1994/Air Control, 1994.
Best-selling record by Da Brat from the album *Funkdafied* (So So Def, 94).

Funky Y-2-C
Words and music by T. Hayes.
No Hassle, New York, 1994.
Introduced by The Puppies (Chaos, 94).

G

Gallows Pole
Superhype Publishing, 1970/WB Music, 1970.
Revived by Led Zeppelin alumni Robert Plant and Jimmy Page on *No Quarter* (Atlantic, 94).

Geography Song
Words and music by Arnold Weinstein, words by Hankus Netsky.
Introduced in *Schlemeil the First*.

Get Off This
Words and music by David Lowery, David Faragher, and John Hickman.
Biscuits and Gravy Music, 1994/Warner-Tamerlane Music, 1994.
Introduced by Cracker on *Kerosene Hat* (Virgin, 94).

Get Over It
Words and music by Don Henley and Glenn Frey.
Black Cypress, 1994/Red Cloud Music Co., 1994/WB Music, 1994.
Introduced by The Eagles on *Hell Freezes Over* (Geffen, 94).

Gin & Juice
Words and music by Snoop Doggy Dogg (pseudonym for Calvin Broadus).
Suge, 1993/Ain't Nothin' Goin on But Fu-kin, 1993.
Best-selling record by Snoop Doggy Dogg from *Doggy-Style* (Death Row/Interscope, 93).

Girl, You'll Be a Woman Soon
Words and music by Neil Diamond.
Stonebridge Music, 1967.
Revived by Urge Overkill in the film and on the soundtrack album *Pulp Fiction* (MCA, 94).

Girls with Guitars
Words and music by Mary Chapin Carpenter.

EMI-April Music, 1994/Getarealjob Music, 1994.
Introduced by Wynonna in *Tell Me Why* (Curb, 93).

Give It Up
Words and music by Gary G-Wiz, Carlton Ridenhour, Studdah Man,
    Alvertis Isbell, and M. Thomas.
Suburban Funk, 1994/Def American Songs, 1994.
Best-selling record by Public Enemy from the album *Muse Sick-N-Hour
    Mess Age* (JAM/RAL; Island, 94).

Glory
Words and music by Liz Phair.
Sony Music, 1992.
Introduced by Liz Phair on *Exile in Guyville* (Matador, 93). Critic's
    choice as Fem-rocker of the year, 1993-94.

God
Words and music by Tori Amos.
Sword and Stone, 1994.
Best-selling record by Tori Amos from *Under the Pink* (Atlantic, 94).
    This follows up her acclaimed work in *Little Earthquakes*.

Golden Feather
Words and music by Robbie Robertson.
Blue Northern, Camden, 1994/Blue Raven, Richardson, 1994.
Introduced by Robbie Robertson and the Red River Ensemble on *Music
    for the Native American* (Capitol, 94). Written for a documentary on
    Native Americans.

Good Enough
Words and music by Sarah McLachlan.
Sony Songs, 1994/Tyde, 1994.
Introduced by Sarah McLachlan *Fumbling Toward Ecstacy* (Arista, 94).

A Good Run of Bad Luck
Words and music by Clint Black and Hayden Nicholas.
Blackened, 1993.
Best-selling record by Clint Black from the film and soundtrack
    Maverick (RCA, 94).

Goodbye to Innocence
Words and music by Madonna and Shep Pettibone.
WB Music, 1993/Webo Girl, 1993/Bleu Disque Music, 1993/Shepsongs,
    1993/MCA Music, 1993.
Introduced by Madonna on *Just Say Roe* (Sire, 94). This song is from a
    collection celebrating pro-choice.

Got Me Waiting
Words and music by Luther Vandross, Heavy D, Pete Rock, and C. L.

Smooth.

EZ Duz It, 1994/Pete Rock, 1994/EMI Music Publishing, 1994/EMI-April Music, 1994/Uncle Ronnie's Music, 1994.

Best-selling record by Heavy D & The Boyz from *Nuttin' but Love* (Uptown/MCA, 94).

Got No Mind

Words and music by Beck Hanson.

Nothin' Fluxin Music, 1993/BMG Music, 1993.

Introduced by Beck on *Beercan* (DGC, 94).

Greatest Star of All

Music by Andrew Lloyd Webber, words by Don Black and Christopher Hampton.

Music by Candlelight, 1993/PSO Ltd., 1993.

Introduced by George Hearn in the musical and on the cast album *Sunset Boulevard* (A & M, 94).

Groove Thang

Words and music by Renee Neufville, Freddie Washington, Patrice Rushen, Charles Mims, Jr., and Sheree Brown.

Ninth Town, 1994/Naughty, 1994/Baby Fingers Music, 1994/Mims, 1994/Shown Breree, 1994/Freddie Dee, 1994.

Best-selling record by Zhane from *Pronounced Jah-Nay* (Motown, 94).

Guns in My Head

Words and music by Matraca Berg and Gary Harrison.

Patrick Joseph, 1994/Maria Belle, 1994/Warner-Tamerlane Music, 1994.

Introduced by Matraca Berg on *The Speed of Grace* (RCA, 94).

H

Hakuna Matata
Music by Elton John, words by Tim Rice.
Walt Disney Music, 1994/Wonderland Music, 1994.
Introduced by Elton John in the film and on the soundtrack album of
    The Lion King (Disney, 94). Nominated for an Academy Award, Best
    Song of the Year, 1994.

Hallelujah
Words and music by Leonard Cohen.
Stranger Music Inc., 1993.
Introduced by Jeff Buckley on *Grace* (Columbia, 94).

Hannah Jane
Words and music by Mark Bryan, Dean Felber, Darius Rucher, and Jim
    Sonefeld.
EMI-April Music, 1994/Monica's Reluctance to Lob, 1994.
Introduced by Hootie and the Blowfish on *Cracked Rear View* (Atlantic,
    94).

Hard Luck Woman
Words and music by Paul Stanley.
Hori Pro Entertainment Group, 1976/Polygram International, 1976/
    Intersong, USA Inc., 1976.
Best-selling record by Garth Brooks from *Kiss My Ass* (Mercury, 94).
    Country interpretation of Kiss classic.

Hard on Me
Words and music by Tom Petty.
Gone Gator Music, 1994.
Introduced by Tom Petty on *Wildflowers* (Warner Bros., 94).

Having a Party
Words and music by Sam Cooke.
ABKCO Music Inc., 1962.
Revived by Rod Stewart on *Unplugged and Seated* (Warner Bros., 93).

He Thinks He'll Keep Her
Words and music by Mary Chapin Carpenter and Don Schlitz.
EMI-April Music, 1992/Getarealjob Music, 1992/Don Schlitz Music, 1992/Almo Music Corp., 1992.
Best-selling record by Mary Chapin Carpenter from *Come On, Come On* (Columbia, 92). Nominated for a Grammy Award, Best Record of the Year, 1994.

Hello Again
Words and music by Michael John LaChiusa.
Introduced by Donna Murphy and David A. White in *Hello Again* (94).

Here Comes a Man (English)
Words and music by Steve Winwood and Jim Capaldi.
Freedom Songs, 1994.
Introduced by Traffic from *Far from Home* (Virgin, 94).

Here Comes the Hotstepper (Jamaican)
Words and music by Ini Kamose, Salaam Gibbs, Christopher Kenner, Domino, A. Kinley, and Kenton Nix.
Salaam Remi, 1992/Longitude Music, 1992/Pine, 1992.
Best-selling record by Ini Kamose from the film and soundtrack album *Pret-a-Porter (Ready to Wear)* (Columbia, 94).

Hey Baby
Words and music by Maggie Estep.
Imago Songs, 1994.
Introduced by Maggie Estep on *No More Mr. Nice Girl* (Imago, 94).
  Poetry stepped center stage in the unplugged era.

Hold My Hand
Words and music by Mark Bryan, Dean Felber, Darius Rucher, and Jim Sonefeld.
EMI-April Music, 1994/Monica's Reluctance to Lob, 1994.
Best-selling record by Hootie and the Blowfish from *Cracked Rear View* (Atlantic, 94).

Hollywood Perfume
Words and music by Chrissie Hynde, Billy Steinberg, and Tom Kelly.
Billy Steinberg Music, 1994/Denise Barry Music, 1994/Clive Banks Songs, 1994.
Introduced by The Pretenders on *Last of the Independents* (Sire, 94).

House of Cards
Words and music by Mary Chapin Carpenter.
Getarealjob Music, 1994/EMI-April Music, 1994.
Introduced by Mary Chapin Carpenter from the Grammy-winning *Stones in the Road* (Columbia, 94).

How 'bout Us
Words and music by Dana Walden.
Irving Music Inc., 1981.
Revived by Mitch Malloy on *Ceilings and Walls* (BMG, 94).

How Can I Help You Say Goodbye
Words and music by Burton Banks Collins and Karen Taylor-Good.
Burton Collins, 1994/W.B.M. Music, 1994/Karen Taylor Good, 1994/
    Reynsong Music, 1994.
Best-selling record by Patty Loveless from *Only What I Feel* (Epic, 94).
    Nominated for a Grammy Award, Best Country Song of the Year,
    1994.

How Many Ways
Words and music by Vincent Herbert, Toni Braxton, Noel Goring, Keith
    Miller, and Philip Field.
Three Boys from Newark, 1993/Polygram Music Publishing Inc., 1993/
    Lady Ashley, 1993/Jay Bird Alley, 1993/Black Hand, 1993/Zomba
    Music, 1993/Raphic, 1993.
Best-selling record by Toni Braxton from *Toni Braxton* (LaFace/Aristic,
    93).

I

I Alone
Words and music by Edward Kowalcyzk, Patrick Dahlheimer, Chad
  Gracey, and Chad Taylor.
Loco De Amor, New York, 1994/Audible Sun, New York, 1994.
Best-selling record by Live from *Throwing Copper* (Radioactive/MCA,
  94).

I Am a Scientist
Words and music by Robert Pollard.
Needmore Songs, 1994.
Introduced by Guided by Voices on *Bee Thousand* (Scat/Matador, 94).
  Indie Phenom's prolific productivity paved the way to a pop
  breakthrough.

I Can't Reach Her Anymore
Words and music by Mark Petersen and Bruce Theien.
Grand Avenue, Nashville, 1993/Ray Stevens Music, 1993.
Best-selling record by Sammy Kershaw from *Haunted Heart* (Mercury,
  93).

I Can't Wake Up to Save My Life
Words and music by Richard Thompson.
Polygram International, 1993.
Introduced by Richard Thompson from *Mirror Blue* (Capitol, 94).

I Don't Sleep I Dream
Words and music by Michael Stipe, Mike Mills, Peter Buck, and Bill
  Berry.
Night Garden Music, 1994/Warner-Tamerlane Music, 1994.
Introduced by REM on *Monster* (Warner Bros., 94).

I Don't Want to Talk about It
Words and music by Danny Whitten.
Crazy Horse Music, 1971.

Introduced by Crazy Horse on *Crazy Horse* (Warner Bros., 71). Re-released in 1994.

I Just Wanted You to Know
Words and music by Gary Harrison and Tim Mensy.
Warner-Tamerlane Music, 1993/Patrick Joseph, 1993/Sony Cross Keys
    Publishing Co. Inc., 1993/Miss Dot, 1993.
Best-selling record by Mark Chesnutt from *Almost Goodbye* (MCA, 93).

I Miss You
Words and music by Gregory Cauthen and Aaron Hall.
MCA Music, 1994/Jamron, 1994/Sweetness, 1994.
Best-selling record by Aaron Hall from the album *The Truth* (Silas, 94).

I Misunderstood (English)
Words and music by Richard Thompson.
Beeswing Music, 1992.
Revived by Dinosaur Jr. on *Beat the Retreat: Songs of Richard
    Thompson* (Capitol, 94).

I Need Love
Words and music by James Todd Smith, Robert Ervin, Steve Ettinger,
    Dewayne Simon, and Darryl Pierce.
Def Jam, 1988.
Revived by Luka Bloom on *In Their Own Words* (Razor & Tie, 94).

I Never Knew Love
Words and music by Larry Boone and Will Robinson.
Sony Cross Keys Publishing Co. Inc., 1993/Wonderland Music, 1993/
    Will Robinsongs, 1993.
Best-selling record by Doug Stone from *More Love* (Epic, 93).

I See It Now
Words and music by Paul Nelson, Larry Boone, and Woody Lee.
Sony Tree Publishing, 1994/Sony Cross Keys Publishing Co. Inc.,
    1994/WB Music, 1994.
Best-selling record by Tracy Lawrence from *I See It Now* (Atlantic, 94).

I Swear
Words and music by Frank Myers and Gerry Baker.
Morganactive Music, 1992/Rick Hall Music, 1992.
Best-selling record by John Michael Montgomery from *Life's a Dance*
    (Atlantic, 92). Revived by All-4-One on *All-4-One* (Blitz/Atlantic,
    94). This rare country/R&B crossover resulted in a pair of hits. Won
    a Grammy Award for Best Country Song of the Year 1994.
    Nominated for a Grammy Award, Best Song of the Year, 1994.

I Take My Chances
Words and music by Mary Chapin Carpenter and Don Schlitz.

EMI Music Publishing, 1992/Getarealjob Music, 1992/Don Schlitz
  Music, 1992/Almo Music Corp., 1992.
Best-selling record by Mary Chapin Carpenter from *Come On, Come On*
  (Columbia, 92).

I Try to Think about Elvis
English words and music by Gary Burr.
Ludlow Music Inc., 1994/Gary Burr Music, 1994.
Best-selling record by Patty Loveless from *When Fallen Angels Fly*
  (Epic, 94).

I Wanna Be Down
Words and music by Keith Crouch and Kipper Jones.
Human Rhythm, 1994/Young Legend, 1994/Chrysalis Music Group,
  1994.
Best-selling record by Brandy from *Brandy* (Atlantic, 94).

I Want Everything
Words and music by David Lowery.
Biscuits and Gravy Music, 1994/Warner-Tamerlane Music, 1994.
Introduced by Cracker on *Kerosene Hat* (Virgin, 94).

I Want to Be Loved Like That
Words and music by Phil Barnhart, Sam Hogin, and Bill LaBounty.
Sony Tree Publishing, 1993/Warner-Tamerlane Music, 1993.
Best-selling record by Shenandoah from *Under the Kudzu* (RCA, 93).

I'd Give Anything
Words and music by Curtis Farren, Jeffrey Steele, and Vince Melamed.
Full Keel Music, 1994/Farrenuff, 1994/Farren Curtis, 1994/Longitude
  Music, 1994/August Wind Music, 1994/Albert Paw, 1994/Mike Curb
  Productions, 1994.
Revived by Gerald Levert from the album *Groove On* (Eastwest, 94).
  Introduced by Boy Howdy as "She'd Give Anything."

I'd Like to Have That One Back
Words and music by Bill Shore, Rick West, and Aaron Barker.
M. Carey Songs, 1993/Hidden Harbor, 1993/Dabi Lu, 1993/Katie
  Walker, 1993/O-Tex Music, 1993.
Best-selling record by George Strait from *Easy Come, Easy Go* (MCA,
  93).

If Bubba Can Dance (I Can Too)
Words and music by Marty Raybon, Mike McGuire, and Bob McDill.
Sugar Bend, 1994/Polygram Music Publishing Inc., 1994/Ranger Bob
  Music, 1994.
Best-selling record by Shenandoah from the album *Under the Kudzu*
  (RCA, 94).

If I Can't Love Her
Music by Alan Menken, words by Tim Rice.
Walt Disney Music, 1994/Wonderland Music, 1994.
Introduced by the original Broadway cast in *Beauty and the Beast* (94).

If I Were a Carpenter
Words and music by Tim Hardin.
Alley Music, 1966/Trio Music Co., Inc., 1966.
Revived by Robert Plant on *Fate of Nations* (Es Paranza, 93).

If That's Your Boyfriend (He Wasn't Last Night)
Words and music by Me'Shell NdegeOcello.
Warner-Tamerlane Music, 1993/Revolutionary Jazz Giant, 1993/Nomad-Noman, 1993.
Best-selling record by Me'Shell NdegeOcello from *Plantation Lullabies* (Sire/Maverick, 93). Nominated for a Grammy Award, Best R&B Song of the Year, 1994.

If the Good Die Young
Words and music by Paul Nelson and Craig Wiseman.
Sony Tree Publishing, 1993/Almo Music Corp., 1993.
Best-selling record by Tracy Lawrence from *Alibis* (Atlantic, 93).

If You Go
Words and music by Jon Secada and Manuel Morejon.
Foreign Imported, 1994.
Best-selling record by Jon Secada from the album *Heart, Soul and a Voice* (SBK, 94).

If You've Got Love
Words and music by Steve Seskin and Mark Sanders.
Love This Town, 1994/MCA Music, 1994.
Best-selling record by John Michael Montgomery from *Kickin' It Up* (Atlantic, 94).

I'll Make Love to You
Words and music by Babyface (pseudonym for Kenny Edmunds).
Sony Songs, 1994/Ecaf, 1994.
Best-selling record by Boyz II Men from the album *II* (Motown, 94). Won a Grammy Award for Best Rhythm 'n Blues Song of the Year 1994. Nominated for a Grammy Award, Best Record of the Year, 1994.

I'll Rise
Words and music by Ben Harper.
EMI-Virgin, 1993/Innocent Criminal, 1993.
Introduced by Ben Harper on *Welcome to the Cruel World.*

I'll Stand By You (English)
Words and music by Chrissie Hynde, Billy Steinberg, and Tom Kelly.
Jerk Awake, Los Angeles, 1994/Hynde House of Hits, England, 1994/
   Clive Banks Songs, 1994/Tom Kelly, 1994.
Best-selling record by The Pretenders on *Last of the Independents* (Sire,
   94). Return of rock's most poignant alterna-legend.

I'll Take You There
Words and music by Alvertis Isbell.
Irving Music Inc., 1972.
Revived by General Public in the film and on the soundtrack album
   Threesome (Epic Soundtrack, 94).

I'm Allowed
Words and music by Buffalo Tom.
Scrawny, New York, 1994.
Introduced by Buffalo Tom on *Red Letter Day* (BMG, 94).

I'm Holding My Own
Words and music by Tony Arata.
Pookie Bear, 1994/Bug Music, 1994.
Best-selling record by Lee Roy Parnell from *On the Road* (Arista, 94).

I'm in the Mood
Words and music by Steven Nikolas, Brendan Sibley, SoulShock,
   Karlin, and Cutfather.
EMI-Virgin, 1994/Casadida, 1994/Steven & Brendan Songs, 1994.
Best-selling record by Cece Peniston from *Thought 'Ya Knew* (A & M,
   94).

I'm Leaving Texas
Words and music by Carole Hall.
Introduced by Dee Hoty in *The Best Little Whorehouse Goes Public*.

I'm Ready
Words and music by Daryl Simmons and Babyface (pseudonym for
   Kenny Edmunds).
Ecaf, 1993/Sony Songs, 1993.
Best-selling record by Tevin Campbell from *I'm Ready* (Qwest/Warner
   Bros., 93).

I'm the Only One
Words and music by Melissa Etheridge.
MLE Music, 1994/Almo Music Corp., 1994.
Best-selling record by Melissa Etheridge from *Yes I Am* (Island, 93).
   Nominated for a Grammy Award, Best Rock Song of the Year, 1994.

In My Next Life
Words and music by Max D. Barnes.

Irving Music Inc., 1994/Hardscratch, 1994.
Introduced by Merle Haggard (Curb, 94).

In the House of Stone and Light
Words and music by Martin Page.
EMI-Virgin, 1994/Martin Page Music, 1994.
Introduced by Martin Page on *In the House of Stone and Light* (Mercury, 94).

In the Name of the Father (Irish)
Words and music by Bono (pseudonym for Bono Vox), Gavin Friday, and Maurice Seezer.
Blue Mountain Music, Ltd., London, England, 1993/Polygram International, 1993/Polygram International Music B.V., 1993.
Introduced by Bono & Gavin Friday in the film and on the soundtrack *In the Name of the Father* (Island, 94).

Independence Day
Words and music by Gretchen Peters.
Sony Cross Keys Publishing Co. Inc., 1993.
Best-selling record by Martina McBride from *The Way That I Am* (RCA, 93). Nominated for a Grammy Award, Best Country Song of the Year, 1994.

Indian Outlaw
Words and music by Tommy Barnes, Gene Simmons, and John Loudermilk.
Edge o' the Woods, 1994/Tommy Barnes, 1994/Great Cumberland Music, 1994/Acuff Rose Music, 1994.
Best-selling record by Tim McGraw from *Not a Moment Too Soon* (Curb, 94). Song many found offensive to Native Americans.

Insider
Words and music by Tom Petty.
Gone Gator Music, 1981.
Revived by Silkworm in *You Got Lucky* (Backyard/Scotti Brothers, 94).

Interstate Love Song
Words and music by Robert DeLeo and Scott Weiland.
EMI-Virgin, 1994/Floated Music, 1994.
Introduced by Stone Temple Pilots on *Purple* (Atlantic, 94).

It Can't Rain All the Time (Canadian)
Words and music by Jane Siberry.
Pressmancherry, 1993/WB Music, 1993/Wing It, 1993.
Revived by Jane Siberry in the film and on the soundtrack of *The Crow* (Atlantic, 94).

It Tears Me Up
Words and music by Spooner Oldham and Dan Penn.
EMI Music Publishing, 1966.
Revived by Dan Penn on *Do Right Man* (Sire, 94).

It's Been a While
Words and music by Carole Hall.
Introduced by Dee Hoty and Scott Holmes in *The Best Little
    Whorehouse Goes Public*.

It's the Same Old Song
Words and music by Eddie Holland, Lamont Dozier, and Brian Holland.
Stone Agate Music, 1965.
Revived by David Wilcox on *Big Horizon* (A & M, 94).

I've Got It Made
Words and music by Max D. Barnes.
Irving Music Inc., 1993/Hardscratch, 1993.
Best-selling record by John Anderson from *Solid Ground* (BWA, 93).

J

Jealousy
Words and music by Liz Phair.
Sony Music, 1994.
Introduced by Liz Phair on *Whip Smart* (Matador, 94).

Jolene
Words and music by Dolly Parton.
Velvet Apple Music, 1973.
Revived by Matraca Berg on *The Speed of Grace* (BMG, 94).

Juicy/Unbelievable
Words and music by The Notorious B.I.G.
Tee Tee, 1994/Janice Combs, 1994.
Best-selling record by The Notorious B.I.G. from *Ready to Die* (Bad Boy/Arista, 94).

Just about Glad
Words and music by Declan McManus.
Plangent Visions Music, Inc., London, England, 1993.
Introduced by Elvis Costello on *Brutal Youth* (Warner Bros., 94).

K

Keep Talking (English)
Words and music by David Gilmour, Polly Samson, and Richard
    Wright.
Pink Floyd Ltd., 1994.
Best-selling record by Pink Floyd from *The Division Bell* (Columbia,
    94). The song features physicist Stephen Hawkings' voice through an
    electronic voicebox.

Kim the Waitress
Words and music by Jeff Kelly.
Endless Moment, Woodinville, 1994.
Introduced by Material Issue on *Freak City Soundtrack* (Mercury, 94).

L

Laid (English)
Words and music by Tim Booth, Larry Gott, Saul Davies, Mark Hunter, Jim Glennie, and David Bayton-Power.
Polygram International, 1993.
Best-selling record by James from *Laid* (Mercury, 94).

Landslide
Words and music by Stevie Nicks.
Rockhopper Music Inc., 1975.
Revived by Smashing Pumpkins on *Pisces Iscariot* (Virgin, 94).

Last Goodbye
Words and music by Jeff Buckley.
Sony Songs, 1994/El Viejito, 1994.
Introduced by Jeff Buckley on *Grace* (Columbia, 94). Son of jazz/rock folkie legend, Tim, made big impact in 1994.

Learn to Be Lonely
Music by Larry Grossman, words by Betty Comden and Adolph Green.
Revelation Music Publishing Corp., 1994/Betdolph Music, 1994/Manor Lane, 1994/Fiddleback, 1994.
Introduced by Jill Gedden in *A Doll's Life*.

Leaving Las Vegas
Words and music by Sheryl Crow, Bill Bottrell, David Baerwald, Kevin Gilbert, and David Ricketts.
Old Crow, Los Angeles, 1993/Warner-Tamerlane Music, 1993/Ignorant, 1993/Zen of Iniquity, 1993/Almo Music Corp., 1993/WB Music, 1993/Canvas Mattress, 1993.
Introduced by Sheryl Crow on *Tuesday Night Music Club* (A & M, 93).

Let It Go
Words and music by Prince.
Controversy Music, 1994/WB Music, 1994.
Best-selling record by Prince from *Come* (Warner Bros., 94).

Let It Snow
Words and music by Brian McKnight and Wayna Morris.
Squirt Shot, New York, 1993/Cancelled Lunch, 1993/PRI Music, 1993.
Best-selling record by Boyz II Men from *Christmas Interpretations* (Motown, 93).

Let Me Be Your Wings
Words and music by Barry Manilow, Bruce Sussman, and Jack Feldman.
Jacquimo, Clare, Ireland, 1993/Don Bluth, 1993.
Introduced by Barry Manilow and Debra Byrd in the film and on the soundtrack album *Thumbelina* (SBK/ERG, 94).

Let's Do It Again
Words and music by Curtis Mayfield.
Warner-Tamerlane Music, 1975.
Revived by The Repercussions on *A Tribute to Curtis Mayfield* (Warner Bros., 94).

Liar
Words and music by Henry Rollins.
Rok Godz, 1994/Imago Songs, 1994.
Introduced by The Rollins Band on *Weight* (Imago, 94). Bravura hard rock performance by the poet overlord of rock.

Lifeguard Sleeping, Girl Drowning (English)
Words and music by Morrissey and Boz Boorer.
Bona Relations Music, 1994/Warner-Tamerlane Music, 1994.
Introduced by Morrissey on *Vauxhall and I* (Sire, 94).

Like a River
Words and music by Carly Simon.
C'est Music, 1994.
Introduced by Carly Simon on *Letters Never Sent* (Arista, 94).

A Little Less Talk and a Lot More Action
Words and music by Keith Hinton and Jimmy Alan Stewart.
Sheddhouse Music, 1993/Polygram Music Publishing Inc., 1993/ Millhouse Music, 1993/Songs of Polygram, 1993.
Best-selling record by Toby Keith from *Toby Keith* (Mercury, 93).

Little Rock
Words and music by Tom Douglas.
Sony Tree Publishing, 1994.
Best-selling record by Collin Raye from the album *Extremes* (Epic, 94).

Live Until I Die
Words and music by Clay Walker.
Linda Cobb, Nashville, 1993/Us Four, Nashville, 1993/Lon Jayne, New

York, 1993.
Best-selling record by Clay Walker from *Clay Walker* (Giant, 93).

Livin' on Love
Words and music by Alan Jackson.
Yee Haw, Nashville, 1994.
Best-selling record by Alan Jackson from *Who I Am* (Arista, 94).

Living in Danger (Swedish)
English words and music by Joker and Buddha.
Careers-BMG, 1993/Megasongs, 1993.
Best-selling record by Ace of Base from *The Sign* (Arista, 94).

Longview
Words and music by Billy Joe.
Green Day Music, 1994.
Best-selling record by Green Day from the album *Dookie* (Reprise, 94).

Look What Love Has Done
Words and music by Carole Bayer Sager, James Newton Howard, James
    Ingram, and Patty Smyth.
Music of the World, 1994/Yah-Mo, 1994/Newton House Music, 1994/
    Pink Smoke Music, 1994/EMI-Blackwood Music Inc., 1994/WB
    Music, 1994.
Introduced by Patty Smyth in the movie *Junior* (94). Nominated for an
    Academy Award, Best Original Song of the Year, 1994.

Loser
Words and music by Beck Hanson and Karl Stephenson.
Nothin' Fluxin Music, 1992/BMG Music, 1992.
Best-selling record by Beck from *Mellow Gold* (DGC, 94). Generation
    X anthem hit the pop Top X.

Losin' It
Words and music by Larry Kirwan.
Starry Plough Music, 1994/EMI-Blackwood Music Inc., 1994.
Introduced by Black 47 on *Home of the Brave* (SBK/EMI, 94).

Love a Little Stronger
Words and music by Chuck Jones, Billy Crittenden, and Gregory Swint.
Great Cumberland Music, 1994/Diamond Struck Music, 1994/Circle of
    Life, 1994/Heart Doctor, 1994/Angelo DeLugo, 1994/Storm Front,
    1994/John Juan, 1994/Ensign Music, 1994.
Best-selling record by Diamond Rio from the album *Love a Little
    Stronger* (Arista, 94).

Love Is All Around (English)
Words and music by Reg Presley.
Songs of Polygram, 1968.

Revived by Wet Wet Wet on the soundtrack and in the film *Four Weddings and a Funeral* (London, 93). Also on *Part One* (London, 94).

Love Sneakin' Up on You
Words and music by Tom Snow and Jim Scott.
Snow Music, 1994/Sony Songs, 1994/Lapsed Catholic, 1994.
Best-selling record by Bonnie Raitt from *Longing in Their Hearts* (Capitol, 94). Nominated for a Grammy Award, Record of the Year, 1994.

Loving You
Words and music by Stephen Sondheim.
Rilting Music Inc., 1994/WB Music, 1994.
Performed by Nancy Wilson and Peabo Bryson on *Color and Light: Jazz Sketches on Sondheim* (Song Classical, 94). Introduced by Donna Murphy in *Passion.*

Low
Words and music by David Lowery, John Hickman, and David Faragher.
Biscuits and Gravy Music, 1994/Warner-Tamerlane Music, 1994.
Introduced by Cracker on *Kerosene Hat* (Virgin, 94).

Low Lights of Town
Words and music by Butch Hancock.
Two Roads, 1994/Bug Music, 1994.
Introduced by Butch Hancock in the musical and on the cast album *Chippie* (Hollywood, 94).

Lucas with the Lid Off
Words and music by Lucas Secon, Audley Freed, Brown, and Zany.
Megasongs, 1994.
Best-selling record by Lucas from *Lucacentric* (Big Beat/Atlantic, 94).

Lucky One
Words and music by Amy Grant and Keith Thomas.
Age to Age Music, 1994/Reunion Music, 1994/Yellow Elephant Music, 1994/Sony Music, 1994.
Best-selling record by Amy Grant from *House of Love* (A & M, 94).

Lullabye (Goodnight My Angel)
Words and music by Billy Joel.
Impulsive Music, 1993.
Best-selling record by Billy Joel from *River of Dreams* (Columbia, 93).

M

Make Up Your Mind
Words and music by Randy Newman.
Randy Newman Music, 1994/MCA Music, 1994.
Introduced by Randy Newman from the film and soundtrack album *The Paper* (Reprise, 94). Nominated for an Academy Award, Best Original Song of the Year, 1994.

March of the Pigs
Words and music by Trent Reznor.
TVT, NYC, 1994/Leaving Home, 1994.
Best-selling record by Nine Inch Nails from *The Downward Spiral* (Nothing/TVT/Interscope, 94).

Mass Appeal
Words and music by Keith Elam and Chris Martin.
Ill Kid, New York, 1994/Gifted Pearl, 1994/EMI-April Music, 1994.
Introduced by Gang Starr on *Hard to Earn* (Chrysalis/EMI/ERG, 94).

MGB-GT
Words and music by Richard Thompson.
Beeswing Music, 1993.
Introduced by Richard Thompson on *Mirror Blue* (Capitol, 93).

Misled
Words and music by Peter Zizzo and James Bralower.
Pez, Old Brookeville, 1994/Fancy Footwork, Roslyn, 1994/W & R Group, 1994.
Best-selling record by Celine Dion from *The Colour of My Love* (550 Music, 94).

Miss World
Words and music by Courtney Love, Kristen Pfaff, Eric Erlandson, and Patty Schemel.
Mother May I, Sherman Oaks, 1994.
Introduced by Hole on *Live Through This* (DGC/Geffen, 94). Courtney

Love emerged from the shadow of her late husband, Kurt Cobain, to create her own legend.

Miss You in a Heartbeat (English)
Words and music by Phil Collen.
Bludgeon Riffola Music, 1993/Zomba Music, 1993.
Best-selling record by Def Leppard from *Retro Active* (Mercury, 93).

Mmm Mmm Mmm Mmm (Canadian)
Words and music by Brad Roberts.
Polygram International, 1993/Door Number Two, 1993/Dummies
    Productions, 1993.
Best-selling record by Crash Test Dummies from *God Shuffled His Feet*
    (Arista, 94). Deep-throated Canadian parable.

The More You Ignore Me, the Closer I Get (English)
Words and music by Morrissey and Boz Boorer.
Bona Relations Music, 1994/Warner-Tamerlane Music, 1994.
Best-selling record by Morrissey from *Vauxhall and I* (Sire/Reprise, 94).

Morning Goodness
Words and music by Butch Hancock.
Two Roads, 1994/Bug Music, 1994.
Introduced by Robert Earl Keen and Butch Hancock in the musical and
    on the cast album *Chippie* (Hollywood, 94).

The Most Beautiful Girl in the World
Words and music by Prince.
Controversy Music, 1994.
Best-selling record by Prince (Paisley Park, 94). Introduced during the
    evening gown competition for the *Miss USA Beauty Pageant*.

Mother
Words and music by Glenn Danzig.
EMI-April Music, 1989/Evilive, 1989.
Revived by Danzig in *Thrall-Demonsweatlive* (American/Reprise, 93).

Moving On Up (English)
Words and music by Mike Pickering and Paul Heard.
BMG Music, 1994/EMI Music Publishing, 1994.
Best-selling record by M People from the album *Elegant Slumming*
    (Epic, 94).

My Ally
Words and music by Victoria Williams.
Mumblety Peg, 1994/Careers-BMG, 1994.
Introduced by Victoria Williams and Dave Pirner on *Loose* (Mammoth/
    Atlantic, 94).

My Life
Words and music by Iris DeMent.
Songs of Iris, 1994.
Introduced by Iris DeMent on *My Life* (Warner Bros., 94).

My Love
Words and music by Porter Howell, Brady Seals, and Tommy Barnes.
Taguchi, Hermitage, 1993/Square West, 1993/Howlin' Hits Music, 1993/
  Edge o' the Woods, 1993.
Best-selling record by Little Texas from *Big Time* (Warner Bros., 93).

N

National Working Woman's Holiday
Words and music by Roger Murrah, Pat Terry, and James Dean Hicks.
Ears Last, Smyrna, 1994/Murrah, 1994/Castle Street, 1994/On the
Mantel.
Best-selling record by Sammy Kershaw from the album *Feelin' Good
Train* (Mercury, 94).

Never Enough
Words and music by Adryan Russ, words by Doug Haverty.
Introduced by Cass Morgan in *Inside Out* (94).

Never Forget You (English)
Words and music by Peter Ham and Tom Evans.
100% Apple, 1975/WB Music, 1975.
Revived by Mariah Carey on *Music Box* (Columbia, 93).

Never Lie
Words and music by Chris Stokes and Claudio Cuen.
Zomba Music, 1994/Teaspoon, 1994/Hook, 1994.
Best-selling record by Immature from the album *Playtyme Is Over*
(MCA, 94).

New Age Girl
Words and music by Caleb Guillotte.
Nag, 1994/Songs of Polygram, 1994.
Best-selling record by Deadeye Dick from *A Different Story* (Ichaban,
94). Featured in the film and on the soundtrack album *Dumb and
Dumber* (RCA, 94).

New Ways to Dream
Music by Andrew Lloyd Webber, words by Don Black and Christopher
Hampton.
Music by Candlelight, 1993/PSO Ltd., 1993.
Performed by Glenn Close in the musical and on the Broadway cast

album *Sunset Boulevard* (A & M, 94). Also performed by George Hearn.

Night in My Veins (English)
Words and music by Chrissie Hynde, Billy Steinberg, and Tom Kelly.
Hynde House of Hits, England, 1994/Billy Steinberg Music, 1994/
    Denise Barry Music, 1994/Clive Banks Songs, 1994.
Best-selling record by The Pretenders from *Last of the Independents*
    (Sire, 94).

No Doubt about It
Words and music by John Scott Sherrill and Steve Seskin.
All Over Town, 1994/Sony Tree Publishing, 1994/New Wolf, 1994/Love
    This Town, 1994.
Best-selling record by Neal McCoy from *No Doubt about It* (Atlantic,
    94).

No Excuses
Words and music by Jerry Cantrell.
Buttnugget Publishing, 1994.
Best-selling record by Alice in Chains from *Jar of Flies* (Columbia, 94).

No More Cryin'
Words and music by Terry McBride and Josh Leo.
Songs of Polygram, 1994/Songs of McRide, 1994/Warner-Tamerlane
    Music, 1994/Hellmaymen, 1994.
Introduced by Terry McBride & the Ride in the film and on the
    soundtrack album *8 Seconds* (MCA, 94).

No More Mornings
Music by Larry Grossman, words by Betty Comden and Adolph Green.
Revelation Music Publishing Corp., 1994/Betdolph Music, 1994/Manor
    Lane, 1994/Fiddleback, 1994.
Introduced by Jill Geddes in *A Doll's Life*.

No One Inside
Words and music by Adryan Russ, words by Doug Haverty.
Introduced by Ann Crumb in *Inside Out* (94).

No Time to Cry
Words and music by Iris DeMent.
Songs of Iris, 1994.
Introduced by Iris DeMent on *My Life* (Warner Bros., 94).

Nobody's Hero (Canadian)
Words and music by Geddy Lee, Alex Lifeson, and Neal Peart.
Core Music Publishing, 1994.
Best-selling record by Rush from *Counterparts* (Atlantic, 93).

None of Your Business
Words and music by Herb Azor.
Sons of K-oss, New York, 1994/Out of the Basement, 1994/Next
  Plateau Entertainment, 1994.
Best-selling record by Salt-N-Pepa from *Very Necessary* (Next Plateau,
  93).

Now and Forever
Words and music by Richard Marx.
Chi-Boy, 1994.
Best-selling record by Richard Marx in the film *The Getaway*. Featured
  on *Paid Vacation* (Capitol, 94).

Now My Heart Is Full (English)
Words and music by Morrissey and Boz Boorer.
Warner-Tamerlane Music, 1993/Bona Relations Music, 1993.
Introduced by Morrissey on *Vauxhall and I* (Sire, 93).

Now or Never
Words and music by Yoko Ono.
Ensemble in *New York Rock*.

Nuttin' but Love
Words and music by Heavy D and Kid Capri.
Kid Capri, 1994/EMI-April Music, 1994/EZ Duz It, 1994.
Best-selling record by Heavy D & The Boyz from *Nuttin' but Love*
  (Uptown/MCA, 94).

O

Objects in the Rear View Mirror May Appear Closer Than...
Words and music by Jim Steinman.
E. B. Marks Music Corp., 1994.
Best-selling record by Meat Loaf from the album *Bat out of Hell II: Back into Hell* (MCA, 94).

On Bended Knee
Words and music by James Harris, III and Terry Lewis.
Flyte Tyme Tunes, 1994.
Best-selling record by Boyz II Men on *II* (Motown, 94).

On Grafton Street
Words and music by Nanci Griffith and Fred Koller.
Ponder Heart Music, 1994/Irving Music Inc., 1994/Songs of Polygram, 1994/Plainclothes Music, 1994/Door Number One, 1994.
Introduced by Nanci Griffith on *Flyer* (Elektra, 94).

One Cool Remove
Words and music by Greg Brown.
Brown/Feldman, 1992.
Introduced by Shawn Colvin with Mary Chapin Carpenter on *Cover Girl* (Columbia, 94).

100% Pure Love
Words and music by Crystal Waters, Teddy Douglas, Jay Steinhour, and Tommy Davis.
Basement Boys, 1993/C. Waters, 1994/Polygram International, 1994.
Best-selling record by Crystal Waters from the album *Storyteller* (Mercury, 94).

Out of Tears (English)
Words and music by Mick Jagger and Keith Richards.
Promopub BV, 1994.
Introduced by The Rolling Stones on *Voodoo Lounge* (Virgin, 94).

P

Pass the Mission
Words and music by Tori Amos.
Sword and Stone, 1994.
Introduced by Tori Amos on *Under the Pink* (Atlantic, 94).

Pay No Mind (Snoozer)
Words and music by Beck Hanson.
Cyanide Breathmint, 1993/BMG Music, 1993.
Introduced by Beck on *Mellow Gold* (DGC/Geffen, 94).

The Perfect Year
Music by Andrew Lloyd Webber, words by Don Black and Christopher
  Hampton.
Music by Candlelight, 1993/PSO Ltd., 1993.
Introduced by Alan Campbell in the musical and on the cast album
  Sunset Boulevard (A & M, 94).

Pickup Man
Words and music by Howard Perdew and Kerry Kurt Phillips.
Songwriters Ink, 1994/Texas Wedge, 1994.
Best-selling record by Joe Diffie from *Third Rock from the Sun* (Epic,
  94).

Picture Perfect Morning
Words and music by Edie Brickell.
MCA Music, 1994.
Introduced by Edie Brickell on *Picture Perfect Morning* (Geffen, 94).

Piece of Crap
Words and music by Neil Young.
Silver Fiddle, 1994.
Introduced by Neil Young on *Sleeps with Angels* (Reprise, 94).

Piece of My Heart
Words and music by Bert Berns and Jerry Ragavoy.

Unichappell Music Inc., 1967/Web IV, 1967.
Revived by Faith Hill on *Take Me As I Am* (Warner Bros., 94).

(Lay Your Head on My) Pillow
Words and music by Timothy Christian, Duane Wiggins, and Raphael Wiggins.
Polygram International, 1993/Tony! Toni! Tone!, 1993/Dango, 1993.
Best-selling record by Tony! Toni! Tone! from *Sons of Soul* (Wing/ Mercury, 93).

Pincussion
Words and music by Billy Gibbons, Frank Beard, and Dusty Hill.
Hamstein Music, 1992.
Best-selling record by ZZ Top from *Antenna* (RCA, 93).

The Place Where You Belong
Words and music by Carl Martin, Trey Lorenz, Darnell Van Rensalier, Marc Gay, and Garfield Bright.
Music Corp. of America, 1994/Gasoline Alley Music, 1994/Vandy, 1994/MCA Music, 1994/Petrol Lane, 1994/G-Spot, 1994/Yppahc, 1994/Sony Music, 1994.
Best-selling record by Shai from the film and soundtrack album *Beverly Hills Cop III* (MCA, 94).

Plane Goes Down
Words and music by Sean McNally.
Introduced by Sean McNally on *Grand Slam! Best of the National Poetry Competition.*

Playaz Club
Words and music by Anthony Forte.
Rag Top, Oakland, 1994.
Best-selling record by Rappin' 4-Tay from *Don't Fight the Feelin'* (Chrysalis, 94).

Player's Ball
Words and music by Andre and Big Boi.
Organized Noize, 1994.
Best-selling record by Outkast from *Southernplayalisticadillacmuzik* (LaFace/Arista, 94).

Please (You Got That) (Australian)
Words and music by Andrew Farriss and Michael Hutchence.
Polygram International, 1993.
Introduced by INXS with Ray Charles on *Full Moon, Dirty Hearts* (Atlantic, 93).

Please Don't Take My Air Jordans
Words by Reg E. Gaines.

Ten G Publishing, New York, 1993/DiLithium Crystal Productions, New York, 1993.
Introduced by Reg E. Gaines on *Please Don't Take My Air Jordan* (Mercury, 93). Another poet of the 90s.

Positively 4th Street
Words and music by Bob Dylan.
Special Rider Music, 1965.
Revived by Lucinda Williams on *In Their Own Words* (Razor & Tie, 94).

Power of Two
Words and music by Emily Saliers.
EMI-Virgin, 1994/Godhap Music, 1994.
Introduced by The Indigo Girls on *Swamp Ophelia* (Epic, 94).

Practice What You Preach
Words and music by Barry White, Gerald Levert, and Eddie Nicholas.
Seven, 1994/Super, 1994/Divided, 1994/Zomba Music, 1994/Warner-Tamerlane Music, 1994/Rampal, 1994.
Best-selling record by Barry White on *The Icon Is Love* (Atlantic, 94).

A Prayer
Words by Lisa Buscani.
Introduced by Lisa Buscani on *Grand Slam! Best of the National Poetry Competition.*

Prayer for the Dying (English)
Words and music by Seal (pseudonym for Samuel Sealhenry) and Isidore.
Beethoven Street, 1994/SPZ, 1994/EMI-Virgin, 1994.
Best-selling record by Seal from the album *Seal* (ZTT/Sire; Warner Bros., 94). Moving lyrics addressed to recovering addicts.

Pumps and a Bump
Words and music by Hammer, Deuce Deuce, Gerald Baillergeau, George Clinton, Jr., Gary Shider, and David Spradley.
Bust It Publishing, 1994/Rap and More Music, 1994/Bridgeport Music Inc., 1994/Southport, 1994/Micon, 1994.
Best-selling record by Hammer from the album *The Funky Headhunter* (Giant, 94).

R

Rainy Night in Georgia
Words and music by Tony Joe White.
Combine Music Corp., 1969/EMI-Blackwood Music Inc., 1969.
Revived by Sam Moore & Conway Twitty on *Rhythm Country and Blues* (MCA, 94). Another merger of country and R&B sensibilities.

Rapture
Words and music by Chris Stein and Debbie Harry.
Chrysalis Music Group, 1980/Monster Island, 1980.
Revived by Blondie on *The Platinum Years* (Chrysalis/EMI, 94).

Regulate
Words and music by Nate Dogg and Warren Griffin.
Suge, 1994/Warren G, 1994.
Best-selling record by Warren G & Nate Dogg from the film and soundtrack album *Above the Rim* (Death Row/Interscope, 94).

Return to Innocence (German)
English words and music by Michael Cretu.
Enigma Songs, 1994/EMI-Virgin, 1994.
Best-selling record by Enigma from *The Cross of Changes* (Charisma/Virgin, 94).

Return to Me
Words and music by Julie Flanders and Emil Adler.
October Project, 1993/Famous Music Corp., 1993.
Introduced by October Project on *October Project* (Epic, 93).

The Rhythm of the Night (German)
English words and music by F. Bontempi, A. Gordon, G. Spagna, M. Gaffey, and P. Glenister.
Intersong Products, 1994/Warner U.K., 1994/Gema, 1994.
Introduced by Corona (East/West, 94).

Ride in Your Slipstream
Words and music by Richard Thompson.

Polygram International, 1993.
Introduced by Richard Thompson on *Mirror Blue* (Capitol, 94).

Right Kinda Lover
Words and music by James Harris, III, Terry Lewis, Ann Bennett-Nesby, and Jimmy Wright.
Flyte Tyme Tunes, 1994/New Perspective Publishing, Inc., 1994.
Best-selling record by Patti LaBelle from the film and soundtrack album *Beverly Hills Cop III* (MCA, 94). Also featured on *Gems* (MCA, 94).

The Right Time (Australian)
Words and music by Dave Faulkner.
Copyright Control, 1994.
Introduced by The Hoodoo Gurus on *Crank* (Zoo/Praxis, 94).

Rock and Roll All Night
Words and music by Gene Simmons and Stanley Eisen.
Hori Pro Entertainment Group, 1975/Polygram International, 1975/Colpix, 1975.
Revived by Toad the Wet Sprocket on *Kiss My Ass* (Mercury, 94).

Rock and Roll Dreams Come Through
Words and music by Jim Steinman.
MCA Music, 1975.
Revived by Meat Loaf in *Bat out of Hell II: Back into Hell* (MCA, 93).

Rock My World (Little Country Girl)
Words and music by Bill LaBounty and Steve O'Brien.
Sneaky Moon, 1993/August Wind Music, 1993/Longitude Music, 1993/Steve O'Brien, 1993.
Best-selling record by Brooks & Dunn from *Hard Workin' Man* (Arista, 93).

Rockaway Beach
Words and music by Douglas Colvin, Jeffrey Hyman, Thomas Erdelyi, and John Cummings.
Taco Tunes Inc., 1977/Bleu Disque Music, 1977.
Revived by General Johnson and Joey Ramone on *Anyone Can Join* by the Godchildren of Soul (Forward/Rhino, 94).

Runaway
Words and music by Jon Bon Jovi and George Karak.
Famous Music Corp., 1983/Simile Music, Inc., 1983.
Revived by Bon Jovi on *Cross Roads* (Mercury, 94).

S

Saints
Words and music by Kim Deal.
Period Music, 1992.
Introduced by The Breeders on *Last Splash* (4 A.D./Elektra, 93).

Secret
Words and music by Madonna and Dallas Austin.
WB Music, 1994/Webo Girl, 1994/EMI-April Music, 1994/D.A.R.P.
    Music, 1994.
Best-selling record by Madonna from *Bedtime Stories* (Maverick/Sire,
    94).

Seether
Words and music by Nina Gordon.
Are You There God It's Me, Chicago, 1994.
Introduced by Veruca Salt on *American Thighs* (Minty Fresh/DGC, 94).

Selling the Drama
Words and music by Edward Kowalcyzk, Patrick Dahlheimer, Chad
    Gracey, and Chad Taylor.
Loco De Amor, New York, 1994/Audible Sun, New York, 1994.
Best-selling record by Live from *Throwing Copper* (Radioactive/MCA,
    94).

Sending My Love
Words and music by Renee Neufville.
Ninth Town, 1994/Naughty, 1994.
Best-selling record by Zhane from the album *Pronounced Jah-Nay*
    (Illtown/Motown, 94).

7 and 7 Is
Words and music by Arthur Lee.
Grass Root Productions, 1967.
Revived by The Ramones on *Acid Eaters* (Radioactive, 94).

Sex Kills
Words and music by Joni Mitchell.
Crazy Crow Music, 1994.
Introduced by Joni Mitchell on *Turbulent Indigo* (Reprise, 94).

Shadow of Doubt
Words and music by Gary Nicholson.
Sony Cross Keys Publishing Co. Inc., 1993/Four Sons Music, 1993.
Introduced by Bonnie Raitt from *Longing in Their Hearts* (Capitol, 94).

Shame
Words and music by John Finch and Reuben Cross.
Unichappell Music Inc., 1994/Mills & Mills, 1994.
Best-selling record by Zhane from the film and soundtrack album *A Low
    Down Dirty Shame* (Hollywood/Jive, 94).

She Can't Say I Didn't Cry
Words and music by Troy Martin, Tony Martin, and Reese Wilson.
Starstruck Angel, 1994/Stroudacaster, 1994.
Best-selling record by Rick Trevino from *Rick Trevino* (Columbia, 94).

She Thinks His Name Was John
Words and music by Sandy Knox and Steve Rosen.
Bash, 1994/Mighty Nice Music, 1994/Blue Water, 1994.
Best-selling record by Reba McEntire on *Read My Mind* (MCA, 94).

She's Not the Cheatin' Kind
Words and music by Ronnie Dunn.
Sony Tree Publishing, 1994/Showbilly, 1994.
Best-selling record by Brooks & Dunn from *Waitin' on Sundown*
    (Arista, 94).

Shine
Words and music by Ed Roland.
Roland/Lentz, New York, 1994.
Best-selling record by Collective Soul from the album *Hints, Allegations
    & Things Left Unsaid* (Atlantic, 94).

Shoot Out the Lights (English)
Words and music by Richard Thompson.
Beeswing Music, 1979.
Revived by Bob Mould on *Poison Years* (Virgin, 94).

Short Dick Man
Words and music by Manfred Mohr and Charles˳ Babie.
Tango Rose, Chicago, 1994.
Introduced by Twenty Fingers (Zoo, 94).

Shut Up and Kiss Me
Words and music by Mary Chapin Carpenter.
Why Walk, 1994.
Introduced by Mary Chapin Carpenter on *Stones in the Road* (Columbia, 94). Nominated for a Grammy Award, Best Country Song of the Year, 1994.

The Sign (Swedish)
English words and music by Joker.
Megasongs, 1992.
Best-selling record by Ace of Base from *The Sign* (Arista, 93).

Sky Blue and Black
Words and music by Jackson Browne.
Swallow Turn Music, 1993.
Introduced by Jackson Browne on *I'm Alive* (Elektra, 93).

Sleeps with Angels
Words and music by Neil Young.
Silver Fiddle, 1994.
Introduced by Neil Young on *Sleeps with Angels* (Reprise, 94). This is a tribute to Kurt Cobain.

Snail Shell
Words and music by John Flansburgh and John Linnell.
They Might Be Giants Music, 1994/WB Music, 1994.
Introduced by They Might Be Giants on *John Henry* (Elektra, 94).

So Much in Love
Words and music by Will Jackson, Roy Streigis, and George Williams.
ABKCO Music Inc., 1963.
Revived by All-4-One on *All-4-One* (Blitz/Atlantic, 94).

Something Already Gone
Words and music by Carlene Carter and Al Anderson.
Al Andersongs, Nashville, 1994/High Steppe, Ventura, 1994/Mighty Nice Music, 1994/Bluewater, 1994/Humble Artist, 1994.
Introduced by Carlene Carter in the film and on the soundtrack album *Maverick* (Atlantic, 94).

Something Else
Words and music by Bob Cochran and Sharon Sheeley.
Money Honey, 1959/EMI Unart Catalogue, 1959.
Revived by Little Richard and Tanya Tucker on *Rhythm Country and Blues* (MCA, 94).

Speak Low
Words and music by Kurt Weill and Ogden Nash.
TRO-Hampshire House Publishing Corp., 1943/Chappell & Co., Inc.,

1943.
Revived by Barbra Streisand on *Back to Broadway* (Columbia, 93).

Spin the Black Circle
Words and music by Eddie Vedder, music by Dave Abbruzzese, Jeff
    Ament, Mike McCready, and Stone Gossard.
Innocent Bystander Music, 1994/Write Treatage Music, 1994/Scribing
    C-Ment Music, 1994/Polygram International, 1994.
Best-selling record by Pearl Jam from *Vitology* (Epic, 94).

Spin the Bottle
Words and music by Juliana Hatfield.
Juliana Hatfield, 1993/Zomba Music, 1993.
Revived by The Juliana Hatfield Three in the film and on the
    soundtrack album *Reality Bites* (RCA, 94).

Spoonman
Words and music by Chris Cornell.
You Make Me Sick, I Make Music, 1994.
Best-selling record by Soundgarden from *Superunknown* (A & M, 94).

Standing Outside the Fire
Words and music by Jenny Yates and Garth Brooks.
Criterion Music Corp., 1993/Escudilla, 1993/Major Bob Music, 1993/No
    Fences Music, 1993.
Best-selling record by Garth Brooks from *In Pieces* (Liberty, 93).

Standing Right Next to Me
Words and music by Karla Bonoff and Wendy Waldman.
Seagrape Music Inc., 1994/Spirit Line, 1994/Longitude Music, 1994/
    New Line, 1994/Screen Gems-EMI Music Inc., 1994.
Introduced by Karla Bonoff in the film and on the soundtrack album *8
    Seconds* (MCA, 94).

State of Mind
Words and music by Clint Black.
Wordy, Los Angles, 1993.
Best-selling record by Clint Black from *No Time to Kill* (RCA, 93).

Stay (English)
Words and music by Mark Stevens and Bobby Khzouri.
Kaptain K, 1994/Tu-Tu, 1994/MCA Music, 1994.
Introduced by Eternal (EMI, 94).

Stay (I Missed You)
Words and music by Lisa Loeb.
Furious Rose, New York, 1993.
Best-selling record by Lisa Loeb & Nine Stories from the film and

soundtrack album *Reality Bites* (RCA, 94). From obscurity to number one, muted lament touched a national nerve.

Stay Awhile
Words and music by Edie Brickell.
MCA Music, 1994.
Introduced by Edie Brickell on *Picture Perfect Morning* (Geffen, 94).

Stay with Me Nora
Music by Larry Grossman, English words and music by Betty Comden, words and music by Adolph Green.
Revelation Music Publishing Corp., 1994/Betdolph Music, 1994/Manor Lane, 1994/Fiddleback, 1994.
Introduced by Jill Geddes and Jeff Herbst in *A Doll's Life*.

Stones in the Road
Words and music by Mary Chapin Carpenter.
Getarealjob Music, 1993/EMI-April Music, 1993.
Introduced by Mary Chapin Carpenter on the Grammy-award winning album *Stones in the Road* (Columbia, 94).

Streets of Philadelphia
Words and music by Bruce Springsteen.
Bruce Springsteen Publishing, 1993.
Best-selling record by Bruce Springsteen from the film and soundtrack *Philadelphia* (Epic Soundtrack, 93). Winner of a 1993 Oscar for Best Song. Won Grammy Awards. Nominated for Grammy Awards, Best Movie or TV Song of the Year, 1994 and Best Record of the Year, 1994.

Stroke You Up
Words and music by Robert Kelly.
Zomba Music, 1994.
Best-selling record by Changing Faces from the album *Changing Faces* (Big Beat/Atlantic, 94).

Stupid Thing
English words and music by Aimee Mann and Jon Brion.
You Can't Take It With You, 1994/Lilyac, 1994/Aimee Mann, 1994.
Introduced by Aimee Mann on *Whatever* (Imago, 93).

Substitute (English)
Words and music by Peter Townshend.
Devon Music, 1966/Fabulous Music Ltd., 1966.
Revived by The Ramones on *Acid Eaters* (Radioactive, 94).

Sukiyaki (Japanese)
Music by Hachdai Nakamura and Rokusuke El, English words by Tom Leslie and Buzz Cason.

Toshiba Music Publishing Co., Ltd., Tokyo, Japan, 1963/EMI Music
Publishing, 1963/Beechwood Music, 1963.
Revived by 4 PM from *Now's the Time* (London/Island, 94).

Sulky Girl (English)
Words and music by Declan McManus.
Plangent Visions Music, Inc., London, England, 1994.
Introduced by Elvis Costello on *Brutal Youth* (Warner Bros., 94).

Summertime Blues
Words and music by Eddie Cochran and Jerry Capehart.
Warner-Tamerlane Music, 1958.
Revived by Alan Jackson from the album *Who I Am* (Arista, 94).

Super Nova
Words and music by Liz Phair.
Sony Music, 1994.
Introduced by Liz Phair on *Whip Smart* (Matador, 94).

Superdeformed
Words and music by Matthew Sweet.
EMI-Blackwood Music Inc., 1994/Charm Trap Music, 1994.
Introduced by Matthew Sweet on *Son of Altered Beast* (Zoo, 94).

Superstar
Words and music by Leon Russell and Bonnie Bramlett.
Stuck on Music, 1971/Delbon Publishing Co., 1971.
Revived by Sonic Youth on *If I Were a Carpenter* (A & M, 94).

Surrender
Music by Andrew Lloyd Webber, words by Don Black and Christopher
Hampton.
Music by Candlelight, 1993/PSO Ltd., 1993.
Performed by Glenn Close in the musical and on the Broadway cast
album *Sunset Boulevard* (A & M, 94).

Sweet Lullabye (English-Australian)
Words and music by Eric Mouquet and Miguel Sanchez.
Celine, 1994/Uncle Don's, 1994/Sony Songs, 1994.
Introduced by Deep Forest on *Deep Forest* (550 Music, 93). World
Music epic broke new ground.

Sweet Potato Pie
Words and music by Domino and Kevin Gilliam.
Chrysalis Music Group, 1994/Cats on the Prowl, 1994/All Init, 1994/
Ghetto Jam, 1994.
Best-selling record by Domino from the album *Domino* (Outburst/RAL,
94).

The Sweetest Days
Words and music by Wendy Waldman, Jon Lind, and Phil Galdston.
Spirit Line, 1994/Longitude Music, 1994/EMI-Virgin, 1994/Kazoom,
    1994/Famous Music Corp., 1994/Big Mystique Music, 1994.
Best-selling record by Vanessa Williams from *The Sweetest Days*
    (Wing/Mercury, 94).

Sympathy for the Devil
Words and music by Mick Jagger and Keith Richards.
ABKCO Music Inc., 1968.
Revived by Guns N' Roses in the film and on the soundtrack album
    Interview with a Vampire (Geffen, 94).

T

Take a Bow
Words and music by Madonna and Babyface (pseudonym for Kenny
    Edmunds).
Ecaf, 1994/Sony Songs, 1994/WB Music, 1994/Webo Girl, 1994.
Introduced by Madonna on *Bedtime Stories* (Maverick/Sire, 94).

Take It Easy
Words and music by Jackson Browne and Glenn Frey.
Swallow Turn Music, 1972/Sun City, 1972.
Revived by Travis Tritt on *Common Threads: The Songs of the Eagles*
    (Giant, 94).

Take Me As I Am
Words and music by Bob DiPiero and Karen Staley.
Little Big Town, 1994/American Made Music, 1994/All Over Town,
    1994/Sony Tree Publishing, 1994.
Best-selling record by Faith Hill from *Take Me As I Am* (Warner Bros.,
    94).

Thanks to You (Canadian)
Words and music by Jesse Winchester.
Fourth Floor Music Inc., 1994/Hot Kitchen Music, 1994.
Introduced by Emmylou Harris on *Cowgirl's Prayer* (Asylum, 93).

That Ain't No Way to Go
Words and music by Ronnie Dunn, Kix Brooks, and Don Cook.
Sony Tree Publishing, 1994/Buffalo Prairie Songs, 1994/Don Cook,
    1994.
Best-selling record by Brooks & Dunn from the album *Hard Workin'
    Man* (Arista, 94).

That's Him
Words by Ogden Nash, music by Kurt Weill.
TRO-Hampshire House Publishing Corp., 1943/Chappell & Co., Inc.,

1943.
Revived by Dawn Upshaw on *I Wish It So* (Elektra,Nonesuch, 94).

(Meet) The Flintstones
Words and music by William Hanna and Joseph Barbera.
Hanna Barbera, Atlanta, 1994.
Best-selling record by The B-52's from the album *The Flintstones*
  (MCA, 94). In the movie the group was known as the "B.C.-52's."

There She Is
Music by Larry Grossman, words by Betty Comden and Adolph Green.
Revelation Music Publishing Corp., 1994/Betdolph Music, 1994/Manor
  Lane, 1994/Fiddleback, 1994.
Introduced by Jeff Herbst, Tom Falantich and Paul Schoofler in *A Doll's
  Life*.

They Don't Make 'em like That Anymore
Words and music by Jeffrey Steele and Curtis Farren.
Farren Curtis, 1994/Full Keel Music, 1994/Farrenuff, 1994/Mike Curb
  Productions, 1994.
Best-selling record by Boy Howdy from the album *She'd Give Anything*
  (Curb, 94).

Thinkin' Problem
Words and music by David Ball, Allen Shamblin, and Stuart Ziff.
New Court, 1994/Low Country, 1994/Almo Music Corp., 1994/Hayes
  Street Music, 1994/EMI-April Music, 1994.
Best-selling record by David Ball from the album *Thinkin' Problem*
  (Warner Bros., 94).

Third Rate Romance
Words and music by Russell Smith.
Fourth Floor Music Inc., 1975/WB Music, 1975.
Best-selling record by Sammy Kershaw on *Feelin' Good Train*
  (Mercury, 94).

Third Rock from the Sun
Words and music by John Greenbaum, Sterling Whipple, and Tony
  Martin.
Major Bob Music, 1994/Rio Bravo, 1994/Stroudavarious Music, 1994.
Best-selling record by Joe Diffie from *Third Rock from the Sun* (Epic,
  94).

13 Steps Lead Down (English)
Words and music by Declan McManus.
Plangent Visions Music, Inc., London, England, 1993.
Introduced by Elvis Costello on *Brutal Youth* (Warner Bros., 94).

This D.J.
Words and music by Warren Griffin.
Warren G, 1994.
Best-selling record by Warren G from the album *Regulate...G Funk Era* (Violator/RAL; Island, 94).

This Is Me
Words and music by Tom Shapiro and Tom McHugh.
Great Cumberland Music, 1994/Diamond Struck Music, 1994/Kicking Bird, 1994.
Introduced by Randy Travis on *This Is Me* (Warner Bros., 94).

This Love Starved Heart of Mine (It's Killing Me)
Words and music by Helen Lewis and Kay Lewis.
Stone Agate Music, 1968.
A re-released song by Marvin Gaye on *Love Starved Heart* (Motown, 94).

Thoughtless Behavior
Words and music by John Gorka.
Blues Palace, 1994.
Introduced by John Gorka on *Out of the Valley* (High Street, 94).

Thuggish Ruggish Bone
Words and music by DJ Uneek and Bone.
Ruthless Attack Muzick, 1994/Dollarz N Sense Musick, 1994/Reenu, 1994.
Best-selling record by Bone Thugs N Harmony from *Creepin On Ah Come Up* (Ruthless, 94).

Tighter and Tighter
Words and music by Tommy James and Benji King.
Longitude Music, 1970.
Revived by Tommy James on *The Solo Years* (Aura, 94).

Time of Inconvenience
Words and music by Nanci Griffith.
Ponder Heart Music, 1994/Irving Music Inc., 1994.
Introduced by Nanci Griffith on *Flyer* (Elektra, 94).

Time Won't Let Me
Words and music by Tom King and Chet Kelly.
Beechwood Music, 1966/EMI Music Publishing, 1966.
Revived by The Smithereens in the film and on the soundtrack *Time Cop* (RCA, 94).

To Daddy
Words and music by Dolly Parton.

Velvet Apple Music, 1977.
Revived by Dolly Parton on *Heartsongs* (Columbia, 94).

Today
Words and music by Bill Corgan.
Cinderful, 1994/Chrysalis Music Group, 1994.
Introduced by Smashing Pumpkins on *Siamese Dream* (Virgin, 93).

Tommy (in Seven Minutes) (English)
Words and music by Peter Townshend, John Entwistle, and Keith Moon.
Track Music, Inc., 1993/Peter Townshend, 1993.
Introduced by The Dumb Rock Coalition (Vital Music, 94). Masterful
    recreation on The Who epic by a gaggle of New York underground
    bands, among them Iron Prostate, Uncle Wiggly, and the Lunachicks.

Tomorrow Comes
Words and music by Edie Brickell.
MCA Music, 1994.
Introduced by Edie Brickell on *Picture Perfect Morning* (Geffen, 94).

Tootsee Roll
Words and music by John McGowan and Nathaniel Orange.
Downlow Quad, Orlando, 1994.
Best-selling record by 69 Boyz from the album *Nineteen Ninety Quad*
    (Rip-It, 94).

Touch Me Fall
Words and music by Amy Ray.
EMI-Virgin, 1994/Godhap Music, 1994.
Introduced by The Indigo Girls on *Swamp Ophelia* (Epic, 94).

Tryin' to Get Over You
Words and music by Vince Gill.
Benefit Music, 1992.
Best-selling record by Vince Gill from *I Still Believe in You* (MCA, 92).

Turn the Beat Around
Words and music by Paul Jackson and Gene Jackson.
Unichappell Music Inc., 1979.
Revived by Gloria Estefan from the film and soundtrack album *The
    Specialist* (Crescent Moon/Epic, 94). Also on *Hold Me, Thrill Me,
    Kiss Me* (Epic, 94).

21st Century (Digital Boy)
Words and music by Brett Gurewitz.
EMI Music Publishing, 1990/Sick Muse, 1990.
Introduced by Bad Religion on *Stranger Than Fiction* (Atlantic, 94).

Twist and Shout
Words and music by Bobby Russell and Phil Medley.
Unichappell Music Inc., 1960/Screen Gems-EMI Music Inc., 1960.
Revived by an alternative all-star cast playing the pre-Beatle Beatles in
the film and soundtrack album *Backbeat* (Virgin, 94).

Two for the Road
Music by Henry Mancini, words by Leslie Bricusse.
Northridge Music, Inc., 1969/WB Music, 1969.
Revived by Betty Buckley on *With One Look* (Sterling, 94) and Karen
Akers on *Just Imagine* (DRG, 94).

U

U Send Me Swingin'
Words and music by Keri Lewis.
New Perspective Publishing, Inc., 1993.
Best-selling record by Mint Condition on *From the Mint Factory*
  (Perspective/A & M, 93) .

U Will Know
Words and music by D'Angelo and Luther Archer.
Polygram International, 1994/Ah Choo, 1994/12 AM, 1994/
  MelodiesNSide, 1994.
Best-selling record by B.M.U. (Black Men United) in the film and on
  the soundtrack album *Jason's Lyric* (Mercury, 94).

Understanding
Words and music by Manuel Seal.
Full Keel Music, 1994/Air Control, 1994.
Best-selling record by Xscape from *Humming' Comin' at 'Cha* (So So
  Def/Columbia, 93).

Undone: The Sweater Song
Words and music by Rivers Cuomo.
E. O. Smith, West Los Angeles, 1994.
Best-selling record by Weezer on *Weezer* (DGC, 94).

Uneasy Armchairs
Words and music by Polly Pen.
Introduced by the cast of *Christina Alberta's Father* (94).

United Front
Words and music by Speech.
EMI-Blackwood Music Inc., 1994/Arrested Development Music, 1994.
Introduced by Arrested Development in *Zingalumundi* (Chrysalis, 94).

Until I Fall Away
Words and music by Robin Wilson and Jesse Valenzuela.
WB Music, 1992/Rutle Corps, 1992/Bonneville Salt Flats, 1992.

Introduced by Gin Blossoms on *New Miserable Experience* (A & M, 92).

V

Vasoline
Words and music by Dean DeLeo, Robert DeLeo, Eric Kretz, and Scott
  Weiland.
EMI-Virgin, 1994/Floated Music, 1994.
Best-selling record by Stone Temple Pilots from *Purple* (Atlantic, 94).

W

Waiting in the Wings (English)
Words and music by Gary Moore and Jack Bruce.
EMI-10, 1994/Jack Music Inc., 1994.
Introduced by BBM on *Around the Next Dream* (Virgin, 94).

Walking Away a Winner
Words and music by Tom Shapiro and Bob DiPiero.
Great Cumberland Music, 1994/Diamond Struck Music, 1994/Little Big
   Town, 1994/American Made Music, 1994.
Best-selling record by Kathy Mattea from the album *Walking Away a
   Winner* (Mercury, 94).

The Way She Loves Me
Words and music by Richard Marx.
Chi-Boy, 1994.
Best-selling record by Richard Marx from the album *Paid Vacation*
   (Capitol, 94).

Weak for Love
Words and music by Marybeth Derry and Daniel Lavoie.
Criterion Music Corp., 1994.
Introduced by Daniel Lavoie on the TV Show *General Hospital*. Also
   released as a single (Curb, 94).

What Jail Is Like
Words and music by Greg Dulli.
Kali Nichta, 1994/Ultrasuede, 1994.
Introduced by Afghan Whigs on *Gentlemen* (Elektra, 94).

What More Do I Need
Words and music by Stephen Sondheim.
Rilting Music Inc., 1994/WB Music, 1959.
Performed by Dawn Upshaw on *I Wish It So* (Elektra/Nonesuch, 94).

What the Cowgirls Do
Words and music by Vince Gill and Reed Nielsen.

Benefit Music, 1994/Englishtown, 1994.
Best-selling record by Vince Gill from *When Love Finds You* (MCA, 94).

What's the Frequency, Kenneth
Words and music by Michael Stipe, Mike Mills, Peter Buck, and Bill Berry.
Night Garden Music, 1994/Warner-Tamerlane Music, 1994.
Best-selling record by REM from *Monster* (Warner Bros., 94).

Whatta Man
Words and music by Herb Azor, David Crawford, and Cheryl James.
Sons of K-oss, New York, 1994/Bed of Nails Music, 1994/Next Plateau Entertainment, 1994/Irving Music Inc., 1994.
Best-selling record by Salt-N-Pepa featuring En Vogue from *Very Necessary* (Next Plateau/London, 93).

Wheels
Words and music by Chris Hillman and Gram Parsons.
Irving Music Inc., 1969.
Revived by Marty Stuart on *Love and Luck*.

When Can I See You
Babyface (pseudonym for Kenny Edmunds).
Sony Songs, 1994/Ecaf, 1994/Epic/Solar, 1994.
Best-selling record by Babyface from the album *For the Cool in You* (Epic, 94). Nominated for a Grammy Award, Best R&B Song of the Year, 1994.

When Fall Comes to New England
Words and music by Cheryl Wheeler.
Amachrist Music, 1994/Penrod & Higgins, 1994/AGF Music Ltd., 1994.
Introduced by Cheryl Wheeler on *Driving Home* (Philo, 94).

When Jesus Left Birmingham
Words and music by John Mellencamp.
Full Keel Music, 1993/Windswept Pacific, 1993.
Introduced by John Mellencamp on *Human Wheels* (Polygram, 93).

When Love Finds You
Words and music by Vince Gill and Michael Omartian.
Benefit Music, 1994/Edward Grant, 1994/Middle C, 1994.
Best-selling record by Vince Gill from *When Love Finds You* (MCA, 94). Nominated for a Grammy Award, Best Country Song of the Year, 1994.

When We Dance
Words and music by Sting.
Magnetic Music Publishing Co., 1994/Regatta Music, Ltd., 1994/Irving

Music Inc., 1994.
Best-selling record by Sting from *Fields of Gold: Best of Sting 1984-1994* (A & M, 94).

When You Walk in the Room
Words and music by Jackie DeShannon.
EMI Unart Catalogue, 1965.
Revived by Pam Tillis on *Sweetheart's Dance* (Arista, 94).

Whenever You Come Around
Words and music by Vince Gill and Pete Wasner.
Benefit Music, 1994/Foreshadow Songs, Inc., 1994/Uncle Pete Music, 1994.
Best-selling record by Vince Gill from the album *I Still Believe in You* (MCA, 94).

Where Did You Sleep Last Night
Words and music by Leadbelly.
Traditional.
Introduced by Nirvana on *MTV Unplugged in New York* (DGC, 94).

Where Were You Last Night
Words and music by Frank Christian.
Frank Christian Music, 1982.
Introduced by Frank Christian from *Where Were You Last Night* (Gazell, 94).

Whip Smart
Words and music by Liz Phair.
Sony Songs, 1994.
Introduced by Liz Plair on *Whip Smart* (Matador, 94).

Whiskey and Women and Money to Burn
Words and music by Joe Ely.
Tornado Temple, 1994/Bug Music, 1994.
Introduced by Joe Ely in the musical and on the cast album *Chippie* (Hollywood, 94).

Whisper My Name
Words and music by Trey Bruce.
WB Music, 1994/Big Tractor, 1994.
Best-selling record by Randy Travis from *This Is Me* (Warner Bros., 94).

Whispering Your Name
Words and music by Jules Shear.
Geffen Again Music, 1994/Music Corp. of America, 1994/Funzalo Music, 1994/Juters Publishing Co., 1994.
Introduced by Alison Moyet on *Essex* (Columbia, 94).

Who Holds Your Hand
Words and music by Patty Larkin.
La Martine, 1994/Lost Lake Arts Music, 1994.
Introduced by Patty Larkin on *Angels Running* (High Street, 94).

The Whole World Lost Its Head
Words and music by Cindy Valentine and Jane Wiedlin.
Some Other Music, 1994/Lipsync Music, 1994.
Introduced by The Go-Gos on *Return to the Valley of the Go-Gos*
    (I.R.S., 94).

Who's That Man
Words and music by Toby Keith.
Songs of Polygram, 1994/Tokeco, 1994.
Best-selling record by Toby Keith from *Toby Keith* (Mercury, 94).

Wild Night (French)
English words and music by Van Morrison.
WB Music, 1974/Caledonia Soul Music, 1974.
Revived by by John Mellencamp with Me'Shell NdegeOcello from the
    album *Dance Naked* (Mercury, 94).

Will You Be There (in the Morning) (English)
Words and music by Robert John Lange.
Zomba Music, 1993.
Best-selling record by Heart from *Desire Walks On* (Capitol, 93).

Willing to Forgive
Words and music by Babyface (pseudonym for Kenny Edmunds) and
    Daryl Simmons.
Sony Songs, 1994/Ecaf, 1994/Warner-Tamerlane Music, 1994/Boobie-
    Loo, 1994.
Best-selling record by Aretha Franklin from the album *Greatest Hits
    1980-1994* (Arista, 94).

Wink
Words and music by Bob DiPiero and Tom Shapiro.
Little Big Town, 1994/American Made Music, 1994/Great Cumberland
    Music, 1994/Diamond Struck Music, 1994.
Best-selling record by Neal McCoy from the album *No Doubt about It*
    (Atlantic, 1994).

Wish I Didn't Know Now
Words and music by Toby Keith.
Songs of Polygram, 1994/Tokeco, 1994.
Best-selling record by Toby Keith from the album *Toby Keith* (Mercury,
    94).

With One Look (I Can Break Your Heart)
Music by Andrew Lloyd Webber, words by Don Black and Christopher
    Hampton.
Music by Candlelight, 1993/PSO Ltd., 1993.
Performed by Glenn Close in the musical and on the cast album *Sunset
    Boulevard* (A & M, 94).

With You
Words and music by Peter Himmelman.
Himmasongs, 1993.
Introduced by Peter Himmelman on *Skin* (550 Music/Epic, 94).

Without You
Words and music by Peter Ham and Tom Evans.
100% Apple, 1970/WB Music, 1970.
Revived by Mariah Carey on *Music Box* (Columbia, 93).

Woke Up with a Monster
Words and music by Rick Nielson, Tom Peterson, and Robin Zander.
Consenting Adult, 1994.
Best-selling record by Cheap Trick from *Woke Up with a Monster*
    (Warner Brothers, 94).

Woman to Man
Words and music by Daniel Lavoie, Frank Sposato, and Marybeth Perry.
Criterion Music Corp., 1994.
Introduced by Daniel Lavoie on the TV show *General Hospital*, (Curb,
    94).

The Wrong Man Was Convicted (Canadian)
Words and music by Stephen Duffy and Steven Page.
Baked Cheddar, 1994/WB Music, 1994.
Introduced by Barenaked Ladies on *Maybe You Should Drive* (Sire/
    Reprise, 94).

X

XXX's and OOO's (An American Girl)
Words and music by Alice Randall and Matraca Berg.
Sony Music, 1994/Mother Dixie, 1994/August Wind Music, 1994/Great
  Broad, 1994/Longitude Music, 1994.
Best-selling record by Trisha Yearwood (RCA, 94) from the TV show
  American Girl.

Y

Yes I'm Your Angel
Words by Yoko Ono.
Introduced by Yvette Perry in *New York Rock*.

Yesterday Once More
Words and music by Richard Carpenter and John Bettis.
Almo Music Corp., 1973/Hammer & Nails Music, 1973.
Revived by Redd Kross on *If I Were a Carpenter* (A & M, 94).

You
Words and music by Bob Thiele, Jr., Tonio K. (pseudonym for Steve
    Krikorian), and John Shanks.
WB Music, 1994/Behind Bars, 1994/Pressmancherryblossom, 1994/EMI-
    Virgin, 1994.
Introduced by Bonnie Raitt on *Longing in Their Hearts* (Capitol, 94).

You Better Move On
Words and music by Arthur Alexander.
Painted Desert Music Corp., 1965/Keva Music Co., 1965.
Revived by Chuck Jackson and Mark Knopfler on *Adios Amigo: A
    Tribute to Arthur Alexander* (Razor & Tie, 94).

You Better Wait
Words and music by Steve Perry, Lincoln Brewster, Paul Taylor, Meyer
    Lucas, John Pierce, and George Hawkins.
Paul Taylor, Sherman Oaks, 1994/Ragged Music, Ventura, 1994/Street
    Talk Tunes, 1994/Lincoln Brewster, 1994/Jortunes, 1994/Bob-a-Lew
    Music, 1994.
Best-selling record Steve Perry from the album *For the Love of Strange
    Medicine* (Columbia, 94).

You Don't Know How It Feels
Words and music by Tom Petty.
Gone Gator Music, 1994.
Best-selling record by Tom Petty from *Wildflowers* (Warner Bros., 94).

Popular Music • 1994

You Got Me Rocking (English)
Words and music by Mick Jagger and Keith Richards.
Promopub BV, 1994.
Best-selling record by The Rolling Stones from *Steel Wheels* (Virgin, 94).

You Gotta Be (English)
Words and music by Ashley Ingram and Des'ree.
Sony Songs, 1994.
Best-selling record by Des'ree from *I Ain't Movin'* (550 Music/Epic, 94).

You Know How We Do It
Words and music by Ice Cube and Q. D. III.
Gangsta Boogie, 1993/WB Music, 1993/Deep Technology, 1993/Full Keel Music, 1993.
Best-selling record by Ice Cube from *Lethal Injection* (Priority, 93).

You Left the Water Running
Words and music by Rick Hall, Oscar Frank, and Dan Penn.
EMI-April Music, 1967.
Revived by Dan Penn on *Do Right Man* (Sire, 94).

You Made Me the Thief of Your Heart (Irish)
Words and music by Bono (pseudonym for Bono Vox), Gavin Friday, and Maurice Seezer.
Blue Mountain Music, Ltd., London, England, 1993/Polygram International Music B.V., 1993/Polygram International, 1993.
Introduced by Sinead O'Connor in the film and on the soundtrack *In the Name of the Father* (Island, 94).

You Make Me Feel (Mighty Real)
Words and music by James Tip Wirrick, Sylvester James, Sarah Bernhard, Mitch Kaplan, and Derrick Smit.
Wirrick James Tip, Los Angeles, 1978/Sequins at Noon, Los Angeles, 1978/Borzoi Music, Almeda, 1978.
Revived by Sarah Bernhard on *Excuses for Bad Behavior, Part 2* (500 Music/Epic, 94).

You Mean the World to Me
Words and music by L. A. Reid (pseudonym for Antonio Reid), Babyface (pseudonym for Kenny Edmunds), and Daryl Simmons.
Stiff Shirt, 1993/Warner-Tamerlane Music, 1993/Ecaf, 1993/Sony Songs, 1993/Boobie-Loo, 1993.
Best-selling record by Toni Braxton from the album *Toni Braxton* (LaFace, 93). Nominated for a Grammy Award, Best R&B Song of the Year, 1994.

You Never Even Call Me By My Name
Words and music by Steve Goodman.
Turnpike Tom Music, 1973/Pink Sky, 1973/EMI U Catalogue, 1973.
Revived by Doug Supernaw from *Deep Thoughts from a Shallow Mind*
    (BNA, 94).

You Tripped at Every Step (English)
Words and music by Declan McManus.
Plangent Visions Music, Inc., London, England, 1994.
Introduced by Elvis Costello on *Brutal Youth* (Warner Bros., 94).

You Want This
Words and music by Janet Jackson, James Harris, III, and Terry Lewis.
Black Ice Music, 1993/Stone Agate Music, 1993/Flyte Tyme Tunes,
    1993/Jobete Music Co., 1993.
Best-selling record by Janet Jackson from *janet* (Virgin, 93).

Your Body's Callin'
Words and music by Robert Kelly.
Zomba Music, 1993/R. Kelly Music, 1993.
Best-selling record by R. Kelly from the album *12 Play* (Jive, 94).

Your Favorite Thing
Words and music by Bob Mould.
Granary Music, 1994/Bug Music, 1994.
Introduced by Sugar on *File Under Easy Listening* (Rykodisc, 94).

Your Love Amazes Me
Words and music by Amanda Hunt and Chuck Jones.
Gila Monster, 1994/Great Cumberland Music, 1994/Diamond Struck
    Music, 1994.
Best-selling record by John Berry from the album *John Berry* (Liberty,
    94).

Your Smiling Face
Words and music by James Taylor.
Country Road Music Inc., 1977.
Revived by James Taylor on *Live* (Columbia, 93).

Yvette in English
Words and music by Joni Mitchell and David Crosby.
Crazy Crow Music, 1993/Stay Straight, 1993.
Performed by Joni Mitchell in *Turbultent Indigo* (Reprise, 94).

Z

Zero Willpower
Words and music by Donnie Fritts, Spooner Oldham, and Dan Penn.
Maypop Music, 1994/Donnie Fritts, 1994/Spooner Oldham, 1994/Dan
  Penn Music, 1994.
Introduced by Dan Penn on *Do Right Man* (Sire, 94).

Zombie
Words and music by Noel Hogan and Dolores O'Riordan.
Polygram International, 1994.
Best-selling record by The Cranberries on *No Need to Agree* (Island,
  94). Striking commentary on "the troubles" in Northern Ireland.

Lyricists & Composers Index

Lyricists & Composers Index

Lyricists & Composers Index

Important Performances Index

Songs are listed under the works in which they were introduced or given significant renditions. The index is organized into major sections by performance medium: Album, Movie, Musical, Performer, Revue, Television Show.

Album

Above the Rim
  Anything
  Regulate
Acid Eaters
  7 and 7 Is
  Substitute
Adios Amigo: A Tribute to Arthur
  Alexander
  Anna
  You Better Move On
Age Ain't Nothin' but a Number
  At Your Best (YouAre Love)
  Back & Forth
Ahmad
  Back in the Day
Alibis
  If the Good Die Young
All-4-One
  I Swear
  So Much in Love
Almost Goodbye
  I Just Wanted You to Know
American Thighs
  Seether
Angel of Mercy
  A Father and Two Sons

Angels Running
  Who Holds Your Hand
Antenna
  Pincussion
Anyone Can Join
  Rockaway Beach
Anything Goes
  Do You Wanna Get Funky
Around the Next Dream
  Waiting in the Wings
Back to Broadway
  Speak Low
Back Where It All Begins
  Back Where It All Begins
Backbeat
  Twist and Shout
Bat out of Hell II: Back into Hell
  Objects in the Rear View Mirror May
    Appear Closer Than...
  Rock and Roll Dreams Come Through
Beat the Retreat: Songs of Richard
  Thompson
  I Misunderstood
The Beavis and Butthead Experience
  Deuces Are Wild

115

Deep Forest
  Sweet Lullabye
Deep Thoughts from a Shallow Mind
  You Never Even Call Me By My
    Name
Desire Walks On
  Will You Be There (in the Morning)
DGC Rarities Vol. 1
  Einstein on the Beach (for an Eggman)
Diary of a Mad Band
  Feenin'
A Different Story
  New Age Girl
The Division Bell
  Keep Talking
Do Right Man
  Dark End of the Street
  It Tears Me Up
  You Left the Water Running
  Zero Willpower
Doggy-Style
  Gin & Juice
Domino
  Sweet Potato Pie
Don't Fight the Feelin'
  Playaz Club
Dookie
  Basket Case
  Longview
The Downward Spiral
  March of the Pigs
Driving Home
  Almost
  When Fall Comes to New England
Dulcinea
  Fall Down
Dumb and Dumber
  New Age Girl
The Earth Wants You
  Children of the Future
Easy Come, Easy Go
  I'd Like to Have That One Back
8 Seconds
  No More Cryin'
  Standing Right Next to Me
Eleanor McEvoy
  Finding Myself Lost Again

Elegant Slumming
  Moving On Up
11 Tracks of Whacks
  Down in the Bottom
Essex
  Whispering Your Name
Everybody Else Is Doing It, So Why
  Can't We?
  Dreams
Excuses for Bad Behavior
  You Make Me Feel (Mighty Real)
Exile in Guyville
  Glory
Extremes
  Little Rock
Face the Music
  Dirty Dawg
Far Beyond Driven
  5 Minutes Alone
Far from Home
  Here Comes a Man
Fate of Nations
  If I Were a Carpenter
Feelin' Good Train
  National Working Woman's Holiday
  Third Rate Romance
Fields of Gold: Best of Sting 1984-1994
  When We Dance
File Under Easy Listening
  Your Favorite Thing
The Flintstones
  (Meet) The Flintstones
Flyer
  On Grafton Street
  Time of Inconvenience
For the Cool in You
  And Our Feelings
  When Can I See You
For the Love of Strange Medicine
  You Better Wait
Four Weddings and a Funeral
  Love Is All Around
Freak City Soundtrack
  Kim the Waitress
From a Sympathetical Hurricane
  From a Sympathetical Hurricane
From the Mint Factory
  U Send Me Swingin'

Movie

Musical

128

Awards Index

A list of songs nominated for Academy Awards by the Academy of Motion Picture Arts and Sciences and Grammy Awards from the National Academy of Recording Arts and Sciences. Asterisks indicate the winners; multiple listings indicate multiple nominations.

1994

Academy Award
Can You Feel the Love Tonight*
Circle of Life
Hakuna Matata
Look What Love Has Done
Make Up Your Mind
Grammy Award
All Apologies
All I Wanna Do
All I Wanna Do*
Black Hole Sun
Body & Soul
Can You Feel the Love Tonight
Circle of Life
Come to My Window
He Thinks He'll Keep Her

How Can I Help You Say Goodbye
I Swear
I Swear*
If That's Your Boyfriend (He Wasn't Last Night)
I'll Make Love to You
I'll Make Love to You*
I'm the Only One
Independence Day
Love Sneakin' Up on You
Shut Up and Kiss Me
Streets of Philadelphia
Streets of Philadelphia*
Streets of Philadelphia*
When Can I See You
When Love Finds You
You Mean the World to Me

List of Publishers

A directory of publishers of the songs included in *Popular Music,* 1994. Publishers that are members of the American Society of Composers, Authors, and Publishers or whose catalogs are available under ASCAP license are indicated by the designation (ASCAP). Publishers that have granted performing rights to Broadcast Music, Inc., are designated by the notation (BMI). Publishers whose catalogs are represented by The Society of Composers, Authors and Music Publishers of Canada, are indicated by the designation (SOCAN).

The addresses were gleaned from a variety of sources, including ASCAP, BMI, SOCAN, and *Billboard* magazine. As in any volatile industry, many of the addresses may become outdated quickly. In the interim between the book's completion and its subsequent publication, some publishers may have been consolidated into others or changed hands. This is a fact of life long endured by the music business and its constituents. The data collected here, and throughout the book, are as accurate as such circumstances allow.

A

ABKCO Music Inc. (BMI)
1700 Broadway
New York, New York 10019

Acuff Rose Music (BMI)
65 Music Square West
Nashville, Tennessee 37203

Age to Age Music (ASCAP)
see Geffen Music

AGF Music Ltd. (ASCAP)
30 W. 21st St.
7th Fl.
New York, New York 10010

Ah Choo (ASCAP)
see PolyGram Records Inc.

Ain't Nothin' Goin on But Fu-kin (ASCAP)
see Sony Music

Al Andersongs (BMI)
PO Box 120904
Nashville, Tennessee 37212

Alamo Music, Inc. (ASCAP)
1619 Broadway, 11th Fl.
New York, New York 10019

Albert Paw (BMI)
see Longitude Music

List of Publishers

Alien Music (BMI)
c/o Pete Sears
2400 Fulton St.
San Francisco, California 94118

Alley Music (BMI)
1619 Broadway, 11th Fl.
New York, New York 10019

Almo/Irving
1358 N. LaBrea
Los Angeles, California 90028

Almo/Irving Music (BMI)
1358 N La Brea
Los Angeles, California 90028

Almo Music Corp. (BMI)
360 N. La Cienega
Los Angeles, California 90048

Amachrist Music
PO Box 1770
Hendersonville, Tennessee 37077

American Bible Society
Address Unavailable

American Made Music (BMI)
c/o Little Big Town Music
803 18th Ave., S.
Nashville, Tennessee 37203

AMI (BMI)
1052 W. 6th St., Ste. 350
Los Angeles, California 90017

Are You There God It's Me (ASCAP)
1330 M State St., No. 128
Chicago, Illinois 60610

Armato (ASCAP)
see Irving Music Inc.

Arrested Development Music (BMI)
see EMI Music Publishing

ATV Music Corp. (BMI)
see MCA, Inc.

Audible Sun (BMI)
1775 Broadway, 7th Fl.
New York, New York 10019

Audre Mae Music (BMI)
34 Dogwood Dr.
Smithtown, New York 11787

August Wind Music (BMI)
see Longitude Music

Avant Garde Music (ASCAP)
Box 92004
Los Angeles, California 90009

B

Baby Fingers Music (ASCAP)
c/o Gary L. Gilbert Esq.
Blum, Bloom, Dekom, & Hercott
150 S Rodeo Dr.
3rd Fl.
Beverly Hills, California 90212

Bam Jams (ASCAP)
see Warner-Chappell Music

Clive Banks Songs
Address Unavailable

Denise Barry Music (ASCAP)
see Sony Tree Publishing

Basement Boys (BMI)
see Polygram Music Publishing Inc.

Bash (ASCAP)
see Sony Music

Bed of Nails Music (ASCAP)
see Sons of K-oss

Beechwood Music (BMI)
see EMI Music Publishing

Beeswing Music (BMI)
c/o Gary Stamler
2029 Century Park, E., Ste. 1500
Los Angeles, California 90067

Benefit Music (BMI)
7250 Beverly Blvd
Los Angeles, California 90036

Betdolph Music (ASCAP)
see Notable Music Co., Inc.

Bicycle Music (ASCAP)
8075 W. 3rd St.
Los Angeles, California 90048

Big Mystique Music (BMI)
see EMI Music Publishing

Biscuits and Gravy Music (BMI)
see Warner-Chappell Music

Black Hand (ASCAP)
see Polygram Music Publishing Inc.

Black Ice Music (BMI)
see Flyte Tyme Tunes

Blackened (BMI)
c/o Prager & Fenton
12424 Wilshire Blvd., Ste. 1000
Los Angeles, California 90025

Bleu Disque Music (ASCAP)
see Warner-Chappell Music

Bludgeon Riffola Music (ASCAP)
see Zomba Music

Blue Dandelion (BMI)
see EMI Music Publishing

Blue Northern (BMI)
13 Grove St.
Camden, Maine 04843

Blue Raven (BMI)
PO Box 850634
Richardson, Texas 75085

Blue Water (BMI)
Address Unavailable

Blues Palace (ASCAP)
539 Atlantic St.
Bethlehem, Pennsylvania 18015

BMG Music (ASCAP)
1540 Broadway
New York, New York 10036

Bob-a-Lew Music (ASCAP)
PO Box 8649
11622 Valley Spring Ln.
Universal City, California 91608

Bon Jovi Publishing (ASCAP)
see Polygram Music Publishing Inc.

Bona Relations Music (BMI)
see Warner-Chappell Music

Boobie-Loo (BMI)
see Warner-Chappell Music

Borzoi Music
782 Limerick Ln.
Almeda, California 94501

Bovina Music, Inc. (ASCAP)
c/o Mae Attaway
330 W. 56th St., Apt. 12F
New York, New York 10019

Breaker Maker
see Careers-BMG

Bridgeport Music Inc. (BMI)
c/o Sam Peterer Music
530 E. 76th St.
New York, New York 10021

Brockman Music (ASCAP)
c/o Jess S. Morgan & Co., Inc.
5750 Wilshire Blvd., Ste. 590
Los Angeles, California 90036

Brown/Feldman (ASCAP)
PO Box 4044
St. Paul, Minnesota 55104

Bug Music (BMI)
Bug Music Group
6777 Hollywood Blvd., 9th Fl.
Hollywood, California 90028

Gary Burr Music (BMI)
see Tree Publishing Co., Inc.

List of Publishers

Bust It Publishing (BMI)
c/o Manatt Phelps and Phillips
11355 W. Olympic Blvd.
Los Angeles, California 90064

Buttnugget Publishing (ASCAP)
207 1/2 1st Ave. S.
Seattle, Washington 98104

C

Caledonia Soul Music (ASCAP)
see WB Music

Canvas Mattress
see Almo/Irving Music

Careers-BMG
see BMG Music

M. Carey Songs
see Sony Songs

Cass County Music Co. (ASCAP)
c/o Breslauer, Jacobson & Rutman
10880 Wilshire Blvd., Ste. 2110
Los Angeles, California 90024

Castle Street (ASCAP)
1025 16th Ave. S., Ste. 102
Nashville, Tennessee 37212

Cats on the Prowl (ASCAP)
6247 Arlington Ave.
Los Angeles, California 90043

C'est Music (ASCAP)
c/o Gelfand Rennert & Feldman
1880 Century Park E., Ste. 900
Los Angeles, California 90067

Chappell & Co., Inc. (ASCAP)
see Warner-Chappell Music

Charm Trap Music (BMI)
see EMI Music Publishing

Chi-Boy (ASCAP)
c/o Schwartz & Farquharson
9107 Wilshire Blvd., Ste. 300
Beverly Hills, California 90216

Frank Christian Music (BMI)
c/o Michael Lessor
162 E. 64th St.
New York, New York 10021

Chrysalis Music Group (ASCAP)
9255 Sunset Blvd., No. 319
Los Angeles, California 90069

Circle L Publishing (ASCAP)
c/o Spectrum VII Music
Attn: Otis Stokes
1635 N. Cahuenga Blvd., 6th Fl.
Hollywood, California 90028

Linda Cobb (BMI)
1100 17th Ave. S.
Nashville, Tennessee 37212

Cole-Clivilles Music (ASCAP)
see EMI Music Publishing

Philip Collins, Ltd. (ASCAP)
see Hit & Run Music

Color It Funky
see Zomba Music

Colpix (BMI)
see Sony Music

Columbine Music Inc. (ASCAP)
see United Artists Music Co., Inc.

Combine Music Corp. (BMI)
see EMI Music Publishing

Consenting Adult (BMI)
see Screen Gems-EMI Music Inc.

Controversy Music (ASCAP)
c/o Ziffren Brittenham & Branca
2121 Ave. of the Stars
Los Angeles, California 90067

Copyright Control (ASCAP)
see Bug Music

Coral Reefer Music (BMI)
c/o Gelfand, Rennert & Feldman
Attn: Babbie Green
1880 Century Park, E., No. 900
Los Angeles, California 90067

Core Music Publishing (BMI)
c/o Oak Manor
Box 1000
Oak Ridges, Ontario
Canada

Cota Music (BMI)
see Warner-Chappell Music

Country Road Music Inc. (BMI)
c/o Gelfand, Rennert & Feldman
Attn: Babbie Green
1880 Century Park, E., No. 900
Los Angeles, California 90067

Crazy Crow Music (BMI)
see Siquomb Publishing Corp.

Crazy Horse Music (BMI)
5101 Whitsett Ave.
Studio City, California 91607

Criterion Music Corp. (ASCAP)
6124 Selma Ave.
Hollywood, California 90028

Cross Keys Publishing Co., Inc. (ASCAP)
attn: Donna Hilley
PO Box 1273
Nashville, Tennessee 37202

Mike Curb Productions (BMI)
948 Tourmaline Dr.
Newbury Park, California 91220

D

D.A.R.P. Music (ASCAP)
see Diva One

Def American Songs (BMI)
16 W. 22nd St.
New York, New York 10010

Def Jam (ASCAP)
160 Varick St.
New York, New York 10013

Delbon Publishing Co. (BMI)
c/o Mason & Sloane
9200 Sunset Blvd.
Los Angeles, California 90069

Desmobile Music Inc. (ASCAP)
c/o C. Winston Simone Mgmt.
1790 Broadway, 10th Fl.
New York, New York 10019

Deswing Mob (ASCAP)
see EMI Music Publishing

Devon Music (BMI)
see TRO-Cromwell Music Inc.

Diamond Struck Music (BMI)
see MCA Music

DiLithium Crystal Productions
c/o Philip Damien
452 W. 19th St.
New York, New York 10011

Walt Disney Music (ASCAP)
500 S. Buena Vista St.
Burbank, California 91521

Diva One (ASCAP)
Gelfand, Rennert & Feldman
c/o Michael Bivens
1880 Century Park E., Ste. 900
Los Angeles, California 90067

Dollarz N Sense Musick (BMI)
see Sony Music

Don Bluth
Address Unavailable

Donril Music (ASCAP)
225 W. 129th St.
New York, New York 10027

Door Number One
see Polygram Songs

List of Publishers

Downlow Quad (BMI)
740 Lake Ellenor Dr., Ste. 101
Orlando, Florida 32809

Drop Trou Tunes (BMI)
137-139 W. 25th St.
New York, New York 10001

Dummies Productions
see Polygram Songs

E

Ears Last (ASCAP)
c/o William Terry
3305 Dunn St.
Smyrna, Georgia 30080

East Jesus (ASCAP)
see Warner-Chappell Music

Ecaf (BMI)
see Sony Music

Eden Bridge Music (ASCAP)
Address Unavailable

Edge o' the Woods (ASCAP)
1214 16th Ave. South
Nashville, Tennessee 37212

Edition Sunset Publishing Inc. (ASCAP)
c/o Merit Music Corp.
9229 Sunset Blvd.
Los Angeles, California 90069

Edward Grant (ASCAP)
2910 Poston Ave.
Nashville, Tennessee 37203

EMI-April Music (ASCAP)
see EMI Music Publishing

EMI-Blackwood Music Inc. (BMI)
see EMI Music Publishing

EMI Music Publishing
810 7th Ave.
New York, New York 10019

EMI-10 (ASCAP)
see EMI Music Publishing

EMI U Catalogue (ASCAP)
see EMI Music Publishing

EMI Unart Catalogue
Address Unavailable

EMI-Virgin (ASCAP)
see EMI Music Publishing

End of Music (BMI)
see EMI Music Publishing

Endless Moment (BMI)
13305 NE 171 St., No. 6245
Woodinville, Illinois 98072

Englishtown (BMI)
see Warner-Chappell Music

Ensign Music (BMI)
see Famous Music Corp.

Epic/Solar (BMI)
see Kear Music

F

Fabulous Music Ltd. (BMI)
Division of Chancellor Records Inc.
c/o Ivan M. Hoffman
2040 Avenue of the Stars, Ste. 400
Los Angeles, California 90067

Famous Music Corp. (ASCAP)
10635 Santa Monica Blvd.
Ste. 300
Los Angeles, California 90025

Fancy Footwork (ASCAP)
52 Meadow Ln.
Roslyn, New York 11577

Fiddleback (BMI)
see Valando Group

Floated Music (ASCAP)
see EMI Music Publishing

Flyte Tyme Tunes (ASCAP)
c/o Margo Matthews
Box 92004
Los Angeles, California 90009

142

Foreign Imported (BMI)
8921 S.W. Tenth Terrace
Miami, Florida 33174

Forerunner Music (ASCAP)
1308 16th Ave. S
Nashville, Tennessee 37212

Foreshadow Songs, Inc. (BMI)
P.O. Box 120657
Nashville, Tennessee 37212

Four Sons Music (ASCAP)
see Cross Keys Publishing Co., Inc.

Fourth Floor Music Inc. (ASCAP)
Wirrenberg Rd., Rte. 212
Bearsville, New York 12409

Sam Fox (ASCAP)
5257 Hollister
Santa Barbara, California 93111

Freedom Songs (BMI)
see Warner-Chappell Music

Full Keel Music (ASCAP)
9320 Wilshire Blvd., Ste. 200
Beverly Hills, California 90212

Funzalo Music (BMI)
225 W. 57th St.
New York, New York 10019

Furious Rose (BMI)
500 5th Ave., Ste. 2800
New York, New York 10110

Future Furniture (ASCAP)
see Screen Gems-EMI Music Inc.

G

Gamete (ASCAP)
6242 Warner Ave., No. N12D
Huntington Beach, California 92647

Gangsta Boogie (ASCAP)
see Warner-Chappell Music

Gasoline Alley Music (BMI)
see MCA Music

Geffen Again Music (BMI)
see Geffen Music

Geffen Music (ASCAP)
see MCA, Inc.

Gema
Address Unavailable

Getarealjob Music (ASCAP)
see EMI Music Publishing

Ghetto Jam (ASCAP)
see Chrysalis Music Group

Seymour Glass (BMI)
see EMI Music Publishing

Godhap Music (BMI)
see EMI Music Publishing

Michael H. Goldsen, Inc. (ASCAP)
6124 Selma Ave.
Hollywood, California 90028

Gone Gator Music (ASCAP)
c/o Zeiderman, Oberman & Assoc.
500 Sepulveda Blvd., Ste. 500
Los Angeles, California 90049

Granary Music (BMI)
c/o Linda Clark
P.O. Box 1304
Burbank, California 91507

Grand Avenue (ASCAP)
1707 Grand Ave.
Nashville, Tennessee 37212

Grass Root Productions (BMI)
c/o Arthur T. Lee
4717 Don Lorenzo Dr.
Los Angeles, California 90008

Great Cumberland Music (BMI)
see MCA Music

List of Publishers

H

Rick Hall Music (ASCAP)
PO Box 2527
603 E. Avalon Ave.
Muscle Shoals, Alabama 35662

Hammer & Nails Music (ASCAP)
see Almo Music Corp.

Albert Hammond Enterprises (ASCAP)
c/o Brenner & Glassbert
2049 Century Park E., No. 950
Los Angeles, California 90067

Hamstein Music (BMI)
c/o Bill Ham
PO Box 19647
Houston, Texas 77024

Hanna Barbera (BMI)
Box 105366
Atlanta, Georgia 30348

Juliana Hatfield (BMI)
see Zomba Music

Hayes Street Music (ASCAP)
see Almo Music Corp.

High Steppe (ASCAP)
Fitzgerald Hartley
50 W. Main St.
Ventura, California 93001

Himmasongs (ASCAP)
see MCA Music

Hit & Run Music (ASCAP)
1841 Broadway, Ste. 411
New York, New York 10023

Hook (ASCAP)
see Zomba Music

Hori Pro Entertainment Group (ASCAP)
1819 Broadway
Nashville, Tennessee 37203

Hot Kitchen Music (ASCAP)
c/o James Jesse Winchester
2460 Chemin Corriveau
Canton Magog, Quebec J1X-5R9
Canada

House of Fun Music (BMI)
1348 Lexington Ave.
New York, New York 10128

Housenotes (BMI)
Box 9
Hermitage, Tennessee 37076

Howlin' Hits Music (ASCAP)
PO Box 19647
Houston, Texas 77224

I

Ignorant (ASCAP)
see Warner-Chappell Music

Ill Kid (ASCAP)
Howard Comart, CPA
1775 Broadway, Ste. 532
New York, New York 10019

Imago Songs (ASCAP)
152 W. 57th St.
New York, New York 10019

Impulsive Music (ASCAP)
Gelfand Rennert & Feldman
1301 Ave. of the Americas
New York, New York 10019

Innocent Bystander Music (ASCAP)
207 1/2 1st Ave. S.
Seattle, Washington 98104

Interscope Pearl (BMI)
see Warner-Chappell Music

Intersong Products
Address Unavailable

Intersong, USA Inc. (ASCAP)
see Warner-Chappell Music

Irving Music Inc. (BMI)
360 N. LaCienega Blvd.
Los Angeles, California 90048

J

Jack Music Inc. (BMI)
PO Box 120477
Nashville, Tennessee 37210

Lon Jayne
227 Riverside Dr.
New York, New York 10019

Jerk Awake (ASCAP)
c/o Manatt Phelps & Phillips
11355 W. Olympic Blvd.
Los Angeles, California 90064

Jobete Music Co. (ASCAP)
attn: Denise Maurin
6255 Sunset Blvd.
Los Angeles, California 90028

Jones Fall Music (BMI)
see EMI Music Publishing

Patrick Joseph (BMI)
119 17th Ave. S
Nashville, Tennessee 37203

Joshuasongs (BMI)
see EMI Music Publishing

Ju Ju Be (BMI)
3605 Sandy Plains Rd., Ste. 240-248
Marietta, Georgia 30066

Jumping Cat Music (ASCAP)
see Write Treatage Music

Justin Publishing Co.
see EMI Music Publishing

Juters Publishing Co. (BMI)
c/o Funzalo Music
Attn: Mike's Management
445 Park Ave., 7th Fl.
New York, New York 10022

K

Edward Kassner Music
c/o Herzog & Strauss
1773 Broadway
New York, New York 10019

Kazoom (ASCAP)
see MCA Music

Kear Music (BMI)
1635 N. Cahuenga Blvd.
Los Angeles, California 90028

R. Kelly Music (BMI)
see Zomba Music

Tom Kelly
Address Unavailable

Keva Music Co. (BMI)
c/o Richard Becker
PO Box 144
7 Queen Anne Dr.
Deal, New Jersey 07723

L

La Martine (ASCAP)
see Windham Hill Records

Lapsed Catholic (ASCAP)
see Sony Music

Leaving Home (ASCAP)
see TVT

Lilyac (ASCAP)
c/o Patrick Rains & Assoc.
9034 Sunset Blvd., Ste. 250
Los Angeles, California 90069

Lipsync Music (ASCAP)
c/o Nick Ben-Meir, C.P.A.
644 N. Doheny Dr.
Los Angeles, California 90069

Little Big Town (BMI)
see MCA Music

Little Jerald (BMI)
see Warner-Chappell Music

145

List of Publishers

Lla-Mann
c/o Chappell
9000 Sunset Blvd.
Los Angeles, California 90069

Loco De Amor (BMI)
1775 Broadway
New York, New York 10019

Longitude Music (BMI)
c/o Windswept Pacific Entertainment
9320 Wilshire Blvd., Ste. 200
Beverly Hills, California 91212

Lost Lake Arts Music (ASCAP)
c/o Windham Hill Records
75 Willow Rd.
Menlo Park, California 94025

Lucky Nakedress (BMI)
2604 Euclid Ave.
Austin, Texas 78704

Ludlow Music Inc. (BMI)
10 Columbus Circle, Ste. 1406
New York, New York 10019

M

Maclen Music Inc. (BMI)
see ATV Music Corp.

Magnetic Music Publishing Co. (ASCAP)
5 Jones St., Apt. 4
New York, New York 10014

Major Bob Music (ASCAP)
1109 17th Ave. S
Nashville, Tennessee 37212

Aimee Mann
see You Can't Take It With You

E. B. Marks Music Corp. (BMI)
see Alley Music

Dave Mason Music (BMI)
see EMI-Blackwood Music Inc.

Maverick (ASCAP)
see Warner-Chappell Music

Maypop Music (BMI)
Box 121192e Cavender
702 18th Ave.
Nashville, Tennessee 37212

MCA, Inc. (ASCAP)
1755 Broadway, 8th Fl.
New York, New York 10019

MCA Music (ASCAP)
1755 Broadway
New York, New York 10019

Me Good Music (ASCAP)
see Almo Music Corp.

Meat Puppets (BMI)
Box 110
Tempe, Arizona 85281

Megasongs
see BMG Music

Middle C (ASCAP)
Address Unavailable

Mighty Nice Music (BMI)
see Polygram Music Publishing Inc.

Millhouse Music (BMI)
see Polygram Music Publishing Inc.

Mills & Mills (ASCAP)
c/o Chappell & Co., Inc.
810 7th Ave.
New York, New York 10019

Minotaur
Address Unavailable

MLE Music (ASCAP)
see Almo Music Corp.

Morganactive Music (ASCAP)
c/o Dennis Morgan
1800 Grand Ave.
Nashville, Tennessee 37212

Mumblety Peg (BMI)
see BMG Music

146

Murrah (BMI)
   1025 16th Ave. South, Ste. 102
   PO Box 121623
   Nashville, Tennessee 37212

Music by Candlelight (ASCAP)
   see Peer-Southern Organization

Music Corp. of America (BMI)
   see MCA Music

Music Hill (BMI)
   54 Music Sq. East, Ste. 202
   Nashville, Tennessee 37203

Music of the World (BMI)
   8857 W. Olympic Blvd.
   Beverly Hills, California 90210

Musical Moments
   Address Unavailable

N

Naughty (ASCAP)
   see Jobete Music Co.

Needmore Songs (BMI)
   Address Unavailable

New Perspective Publishing, Inc. (ASCAP)
   see Avant Garde Music

Randy Newman Music (ASCAP)
   c/o Gelfand, Rennert & Feldman
   1880 Century Park, E., Ste. 900
   Los Angeles, California 90067

Newton House Music (ASCAP)
   c/o E.G. Music
   9157 Sunset Blvd.
   Los Angeles, California 90069

Next Plateau Entertainment (ASCAP)
   1650 Broadway
   New York, New York 10019

Kali Nichta (BMI)
   Address Unavailable

Night Garden Music (BMI)
   see Warner-Chappell Music

No Fences Music (BMI)
   see EMI Music Publishing

No Hassle (ASCAP)
   c/o Mayer Nussbaum Katz & Baker
   75 Rockefeller Plaza
   New York, New York 10019

Nomad-Noman (BMI)
   see Warner-Chappell Music

Northern Music Corp. (ASCAP)
   c/o MCA Music
   445 Park Ave.
   New York, New York 10022

Northridge Music, Inc. (ASCAP)
   8370 Wilshire Blvd.
   Beverly Hills, California 90211

Notable Music Co., Inc. (ASCAP)
   Cy Coleman Enterprises
   200 W. 54th St.
   New York, New York 10019

Nothin' Fluxin Music (ASCAP)
   see BMG Music

Nuages Artists Music Ltd. (ASCAP)
   see Almo Music Corp.

O

O-Tex Music (BMI)
   see Zomba Music

October Project (ASCAP)
   see Famous Music Corp.

Old Crow (BMI)
   10585 Santa Monica Blvd.
   Los Angeles, California 90025

On the Mantel (ASCAP)
   see Ears Last

Open Secret (ASCAP)
   PO Box 46037
   Los Angeles, California 90046

Organized Noize
   Address Unavailable

List of Publishers

Out of the Basement (ASCAP)
see Next Plateau Entertainment

P

Martin Page Music (ASCAP)
see EMI Music Publishing

Painted Desert Music Corp. (BMI)
10 E. 53rd St.
New York, New York 10022

Peer-Southern Organization (ASCAP)
810 7th Ave.
New York, New York 10019

Penrod & Higgins (ASCAP)
95 Hathaway St.
Providence, Rhode Island 02907

Period Music
see Zomba Music

Pez (BMI)
9 Dolly Corn Ln.
Old Brookeville, New York 11545

Pine
Address Unavailable

Pink Floyd Ltd.
Address Unavailable

Pink Smoke Music (BMI)
see EMI Music Publishing

Polygram International (ASCAP)
1416 N. LaBrea Ave.
Los Angeles, California 90028

Polygram International Music B.V.
Address Unavailable

Polygram Music Publishing Inc. (ASCAP)
Attn: Brian Kelleher
c/o Polygram Records Inc.
810 7th Ave.
New York, New York 10019

PolyGram Records Inc. (ASCAP)
810 7th Ave.
New York, New York 10019

Polygram Songs (BMI)
810 7th Ave.
New York, New York 10019

Ponder Heart Music (BMI)
see Almo Music Corp.

Pookie Bear (ASCAP)
PO Box 121242
Nashville, Tennessee 37212

Portrait-Solar (BMI)
see Sony Songs

Post Oak (BMI)
see Sony Tree Publishing

Pressmancherry (ASCAP)
see Warner-Chappell Music

Pressmancherryblossom (BMI)
see Warner-Chappell Music

PRI Music (ASCAP)
see Polygram Music Publishing Inc.

Promopub BV
Address Unavailable

PSO Ltd. (ASCAP)
see Peer-Southern Organization

R

Rag Top (BMI)
9820 Lindhurst St.
Oakland, California 94603

Ragged Music
299 Arnett Ave.
Ventura, California 93003

Ranger Bob Music (ASCAP)
see Polygram Music Publishing Inc.

Rap and More Music (BMI)
c/o Manatt, Phelps, Rothenberg
& Philips
11355 W. Olympic Blvd.
Los Angeles, California 90064

148

List of Publishers

Realsongs (ASCAP)
Attn: Diane Warren
6363 Sunset Blvd., Ste. 810
Hollywood, California 90028

Red Cloud Music Co. (ASCAP)
15250 Ventura Blvd.
Penthouse 1220
Sherman Oaks, California 91403

Regatta Music, Ltd.
c/o Phillips Gold & Co.
1140 Avenue of the Americas
New York, New York 10036

Reunion Music (ASCAP)
see EMI Music Publishing

Revelation Music Publishing Corp. (ASCAP)
444 Madison Ave.
Ste. 2904
New York, New York 10022

Reynsong Music (BMI)
215 E. Wentworth Ave.
West St. Paul, Minnesota 55118

Rilting Music Inc. (ASCAP)
1270 Ave. of the Americas
Ste. 2110
New York, New York 10020

Rio Bravo (BMI)
see Major Bob Music

Rockhopper Music Inc. (ASCAP)
see WB Music

Rok Godz (ASCAP)
PO Box 1910
Los Angeles, California 90028

Roland/Lentz (ASCAP)
c/o Roland Vasquez
924 W. End Ave., Ste. 1
New York, New York 10025

Ruthless Attack Muzick (ASCAP)
3126 Locust Ridge Circle
Valencia, California 91354

Rye Songs (BMI)
see Sony Music

S

Saja Music Co. (BMI)
see Warner-Chappell Music

Salley Gardens (BMI)
810 7th Ave.
New York, New York 10019

Don Schlitz Music (ASCAP)
PO Box 120594
Nashville, Tennessee 37212

Scrawny (BMI)
810 7th Ave.
New York, New York 10019

Screen Gems-EMI Music Inc. (BMI)
6255 Sunset Blvd., 12th Fl.
Hollywood, California 90028

Scribing C-Ment Music (ASCAP)
see Write Treatage Music

Seagrape Music Inc. (BMI)
c/o Jess S. Morgan & Co.
5750 Wilshire Blvd., Ste. 590
Los Angeles, California 90036

Seasons Music Co. (ASCAP)
c/o Peter Bennett
9060 Santa Monica Blvd., Ste. 300
Los Angeles, California 90069

Sequins at Noon (ASCAP)
1925 Century Park E., Ste. 1260
Los Angeles, California 90067

Erick Sermon
see Warner-Chappell Music

Sheddhouse Music (ASCAP)
1710 Roy Acuff Pl.
Nashville, Tennessee 37203

Shepsongs (ASCAP)
see MCA Music

149

List of Publishers

Shipwreck (BMI)
  c/o Ellen Shipley
  55 3rd Pl.
  Brooklyn, New York 11231

Sick Muse
  see EMI Music Publishing

Silver Fiddle (ASCAP)
  c/o Segel & Goldman Inc.
  9200 Sunset Blvd., Ste. 1000
  Los Angeles, California 90069

Simile Music, Inc. (BMI)
  see Famous Music Corp.

Siquomb Publishing Corp. (BMI)
  c/o Segel & Goldman Inc.
  9348 Santa Monica Blvd.
  Beverly Hills, California 90210

E. O. Smith (BMI)
  1990 Bundy Dr., Ste. 200
  West Los Angeles, California 90025

Snow Music
  c/o Jess Morgan & Co., Inc.
  6420 Wilshire Blvd., 19th Fl.
  Los Angeles, California 90048

So So Def Music (ASCAP)
  see EMI Music Publishing

Some Other Music
  see Lipsync Music

Songs of Iris
  see Forerunner Music

Songs of Polygram (BMI)
  see Polygram International

Songwriters Ink (BMI)
  see Texas Wedge

Sons of K-oss (ASCAP)
  c/o CD Enterprises
  PO Box 650, Church St. Sta.
  New York, New York 10008

Sony Cross Keys Publishing Co. Inc.
  c/o Donna Hilley
  PO Box 1273
  Nashville, Tennessee 37202

Sony Music (ASCAP)
  550 Madison Ave.
  New York, New York 10022

Sony Songs (BMI)
  see Sony Music

Sony Tree Publishing (BMI)
  1111 16th Ave. S.
  Nashville, Tennessee 37212

Special Rider Music (ASCAP)
  PO Box 860, Cooper Sta.
  New York, New York 10276

Bruce Springsteen Publishing (ASCAP)
  c/o Jon Landau Management, Inc.
  Attn: Barbara Carr
  136 E. 57th St., No. 1202
  New York, New York 10021

Square West (ASCAP)
  see Howlin' Hits Music

Squirt Shot (BMI)
  15 Columbus Circle
  New York, New York 10023-7799

Starry Plough Music (BMI)
  31-33 Mercer St.
  Apt. 2C
  New York, New York 10013

Stay Straight (BMI)
  see Hit & Run Music

Billy Steinberg Music (ASCAP)
  see Sony Tree Publishing

Steven & Brendan Songs
  Address Unavailable

Ray Stevens Music (BMI)
  1707 Grand Ave.
  Nashville, Tennessee 37212

Stone Agate Music (ASCAP)
see Jobete Music Co.

Stonebridge Music (ASCAP)
see Bicycle Music

Stranger Music Inc. (BMI)
c/o Machat & Kronfeld
1501 Broadway, 30th Fl.
New York, New York 10036

Street Talk Tunes
Manatt, Phelps, Rothenberg & Tunney
11355 W. Olympic Blvd.
Los Angeles, California 90064

Stroudavarious Music (ASCAP)
see Warner-Chappell Music

Suge (BMI)
see Sony Music

Super Supa Songs (ASCAP)
see MCA Music

Superhype Publishing (ASCAP)
see Walden Music, Inc.

Swag Song Music (ASCAP)
5 Bigelow St.
Cambridge, Massachusetts 02129

Swallow Turn Music (ASCAP)
c/o Manatt, Phelps, Rothenberg
& Phillips
11355 W. Olympic Blvd.
Los Angeles, California 90064

Sword and Stone (ASCAP)
10209 Gary Rd.
Potomac, Maryland 20854

T

T-Boy Music Publishing Co., Inc. (ASCAP)
c/o Lipservices
1841 Broadway
New York, New York 10023

Taco Tunes Inc. (ASCAP)
c/o Overland Productions
1775 Broadway
New York, New York 10019

Taguchi (ASCAP)
5333 Roxborough Pass
Hermitage, Tennessee 37076

Tango Rose (ASCAP)
20 N. Clark St., Ste. 2300
Chicago, Illinois 60602

Paul Taylor (BMI)
14724 Ventura Blvd., Ste. 1007
Sherman Oaks, California 91403

Taylor Rhodes Music (ASCAP)
210 Lauderdale Rd.
Nashville, Tennessee 37205

Ten G Publishing
93 MacDougal St.
New York, New York 10022

Texas Wedge (ASCAP)
37 Music Sq. E
Nashville, Tennessee 37203

They Might Be Giants Music (ASCAP)
232 N. 5th St.
Brooklyn, New York 11211

Tokeco (BMI)
see Polygram Music Publishing Inc.

Tony! Toni! Tone! (ASCAP)
see PRI Music

Peter Townshend
Address Unavailable

Track Music, Inc. (BMI)
c/o Mel Epstein, C.P.A.
130 W. 57th St.
New York, New York 10019

Traditional
Address Unavailable

Tree Publishing Co., Inc. (BMI)
see Sony Tree Publishing

List of Publishers

Trio Music Co., Inc. (BMI)
c/o Leiber & Stoller
9000 Sunset Blvd., Ste. 1107
Los Angeles, California 90069

TRO-Cromwell Music Inc. (ASCAP)
11 W. 19th St.
New York, New York 10010

TRO-Hampshire House Publishing Corp.
(ASCAP)
10 Columbus Circle, Ste. 1460
New York, New York 10019

Troutman's (BMI)
Lefrak-Moelis Ent. Group
40 W. 57th St., Ste. 510
New York, New York 10019

Turnpike Tom Music (ASCAP)
see United Artists Music Co., Inc.

TVT (ASCAP)
23 E. 4th St.
NYC, New York 10003

U

Ultrasuede (BMI)
Address Unavailable

Uncle Pete Music (BMI)
Box 161
Brentwood, Tennessee 37024

Uncle Ronnie's Music (ASCAP)
c/o Padell, nadell, Fine,
Weinburger & Co.
1775 Broadway
New York, New York 10019

Unichappell Music Inc. (BMI)
see Warner-Chappell Music

United Artists Music Co., Inc.
6753 Hollywood Blvd.
Los Angeles, California 90028

Us Four (BMI)
1000 18th Ave. S.
Nashville, Tennessee 37212

V

Valando Group (BMI)
1233 Avenue of the Americas
New York, New York 10036

Varry White Music (ASCAP)
6607 Sunset Blvd.
Los Angeles, California 90028

Velvet Apple Music (BMI)
c/o Gelfand
1880 Century Park E., Ste. 900
Los Angeles, California 90067

W

W & R Group (BMI)
see Fancy Footwork

Walden Music, Inc. (ASCAP)
see Warner-Chappell Music

Wally World (ASCAP)
see Warner-Chappell Music

Warner-Chappell Music (ASCAP)
10585 Santa Monica Blvd.
Los Angeles, California 90025

Warner-Tamerlane Music (BMI)
see Warner-Chappell Music

Warner U.K.
Address Unavailable

WB Music (ASCAP)
10585 Santa Monica Blvd.
Los Angeles, California 90025

W.B.M. Music (SESAC)
see Warner-Chappell Music

Web IV (BMI)
2107 Faulkner Rd. NE
Atlanta, Georgia 30324

Webo Girl (ASCAP)
see House of Fun Music

Wet Sprocket Songs (ASCAP)
901 3rd St.
Ste. 407
Santa Monica, California 90403

Why Walk (BMI)
Address Unavailable

Windham Hill Records
75 Willow Rd.
Menlo Park, California 94025

Windover Lake Songs (ASCAP)
c/o Manatt Phelps & Phillips
11355 West Olympic Blvd.
Los Angles, California 90064

Windswept Pacific (ASCAP)
4450 Lakeside Dr., Ste. 200
Burbank, California 91505

Wing It
Address Unavailable

Wirrick James Tip (ASCAP)
c/o K Music
2555 Hyler Ave.
Los Angeles, California 90041

Wonderland Music (BMI)
see Walt Disney Music

Wordy (ASCAP)
c/o Prager & Fenton
12424 Wilshire Blvd., Ste. 1000
Los Angles, California 90025

Write Treatage Music (ASCAP)
207 1/2 1st Ave. S.
Seattle, Washington 98104

Y

Yah-Mo (BMI)
see Warner-Chappell Music

Yee Haw (ASCAP)
c/o Debbie Doebler
48 Music Square E.
Nashville, Tennessee 37203

Yellow Elephant Music
see Sony Music

You Can't Take It With You (ASCAP)
9034 Sunset Blvd., Ste. 250
Los Angeles, California 90069

You Make Me Sick, I Make Music (ASCAP)
c/o Manatt Phelps Rothenberg &
Tunney
11355 W. Olympic Blvd.
Los Angeles, California 90064

Z

Eric Zanetis (BMI)
370 Peabody St., Apt. 210
Nashville, Tennessee 37210

Zen of Iniquity (ASCAP)
see Almo Music Corp.

Zomba Music (ASCAP)
137-139 W. 25th St., 8th Fl.
New York, New York 10001

ISBN 0-8103-9057-4

90000